Cycling in the
South West
of England
John Grimshaw CBE

AA

Commissioning Editor: Paul Mitchell
Senior Editor: Donna Wood
Senior Designer: Phil Barfoot
Copy Editor: Helen Ridge
Proofreader: Jennifer Wood
Picture Researchers: Alice Earle (AA)
and Jonathan Bewley (Sustrans)
Image retouching and internal repro:
Sarah Montgomery and James Tims
Cartography provided by the Mapping Services
Department of AA Publishing from data supplied by
Richard Sanders and Sustrans mapping team
Researched and written by: Lindsey Ryle, Melissa
Henry, Julian Hunt
Supplementary text: Nick Cotton, Tim Musk
Production: Lorraine Taylor

This product includes mapping data licensed from the Ordnance Survey® with the permission of the Controller of Her Majesty's Stationery Office. © Crown Copyright 2010. All rights reserved. Licence number 100021153.

Produced by AA Publishing
© Copyright AA Media Limited 2010
ISBN: 978-0-7495-6177-2 and
(SS) 978-0-7495-6536-7

Published by AA Publishing (a trading name of AA Media Limited, whose registered office is Fanum House, Basing View, Basingstoke RG21 4EA; registered number 06112600).

A04068

Free cycling permits are required on some British Waterways canal towpaths. Visit www.waterscape.com or call 0845 671 5530.

The National Cycle Network has been made possible by the support and co-operation of hundreds of organisations and thousands of individuals, including: local authorities and councils, central governments and their agencies, the National Lottery, landowners, utility and statutory bodies, countryside and regeneration bodies, the Landfill Communities Fund, other voluntary organisations, Charitable Trusts and Foundations, the cycle trade and industry, corporate sponsors, community organisations and Sustrans' Supporters. Sustrans would also like to extend thanks to the thousands of volunteers who generously contribute their time to looking after their local sections of the Network.

We have taken all reasonable steps to ensure that the cycle rides in this book are safe and achievable by people with a reasonable level of fitness. However, all outdoor activities involve a degree of risk and the publishers accept no responsibility for any injuries caused to readers while following these cycle rides.

The contents of this book are believed correct at the time of printing. Nevertheless, the publishers cannot be held responsible for any errors or omissions or for changes in the details given in this book or for the consequences of any reliance on the information provided by the same. This does not affect your statutory rights.

Printed and bound in Dubai by Oriental Press
theAA.com/shop

Sustrans
2 Cathedral Square
College Green
Bristol BS1 5DD
www.sustrans.org.uk

Sustrans is a Registered Charity in the UK:
Number 326550 (England and Wales)
SCO39263 (Scotland).

CONTENTS

An unplanned adv
in Cornwall

Foreword by **Dr Alice Roberts,** anatomist, author & broadcaster

"You notice much, much more when travelling by bike than you do in a car"

Exactly ten years ago, I set off on a cycling exploration of Cornwall. I like my trips to be unplanned: apart from knowing my starting point, I prefer to let adventures unfold in their own way, and at their own pace, and cycling is one of the best ways to do just that.

So, armed with OS maps, puncture repair kit and chain oil, and a few clothes for all weathers in my panniers, I shut my bike in the guard's van of the train, and travelled down to Plymouth to meet my friend Sue and embark on our pedal-powered adventure.

We caught the Cremyll ferry and headed west. Through a rolling sea mist, we caught sight of the sea at Seaton, then headed inland through a wooded valley, up an unfeasibly long hill. On that first day, our legs were just getting used to the idea – by the end of the journey, we would have thighs of steel! And, despite the best efforts of the English summer, we would be browner, blonder and fitter than when we had started out: the signs of an excellent holiday.

Cycling is both an environmentally-friendly way of getting around – and incredibly healthy. (I obviously cashed in on the health benefits of that cycling holiday, as my diary reads like some *Famous Five* picnic on wheels, with guilt-free chocolate fudge cake in Truro, Cornish ice cream in Mevagissey, spinach-and-feta goujons and more chocolate fudge cake in Marazion, and chips in Padstow).

You notice much, much more when travelling by bike than you do in a car. In Cornwall, I really

enture

Porthcurno beach, St Ives

Lanyon Quoit

appreciated the grandeur of the coastal views, the wildflowers along the verge, coming across cairns and burial chambers, and hearing the clear tones of a blackbird after rain. Memories that stand out particularly from that trip were of strange objects lying at the side of the road, including – bizarrely – bananas and dead fish.

We cycled from Plymouth to Bodmin via St Austell, Mevagissey, Truro, Marazion, Penzance, Mousehole, Porthcurno, Sennen, Hayle, Redruth, Padstow and Wadebridge. It was all unplanned; we found B&Bs wherever we ended up each day, and worked out our route, en route. My diary records the observation that B roads went more up than down, and frequently carried with them the risk of being muck-spread. On A roads, we narrowly avoided coaches full of tourists and being painted with white lines. The only traffic-free route we took was the Camel Trail, and it was wonderful. I wish I'd had a book like this with me at the time, to point us in the direction of quieter roads and cyclepaths. Next time I'll be better prepared!

Of course the National Cycle Network isn't just there for great cycling holidays or day trips. The Network passes within a mile of most of us, and can also make getting to work, school or the shops into a much more pleasant experience – a daily adventure.

St Austell clay works

"The only traffic-free route we took was the Camel Trail, and it was wonderful"

Lobster pots in a Cornish harbour

INTRODUCTION

The South West, with its dwindling peninsula reaching out into the Atlantic, gives a greater sense of Island Britain than perhaps anywhere else in the country. Defined by its coastline, its pretty villages and its friendly country towns, the region attracts those who want to escape an increasingly stressful urban Britain.

Sunrise on Boscombe beach

The South West is home territory for Sustrans, whose head office is in Bristol. We came into being as a sustainable transport charity in 1977 at a time when cycling had been all but abandoned as a way for people to get around. We looked across the Channel to Denmark, Sweden, Germany and the Netherlands and saw something of a renaissance in cycling which we wanted to see emulated here.

So we took the decision to create wonderful routes to demonstrate that people will cycle if provided with the right environment – one that enables people of all ages and ability to cycle more or begin cycling, whether for leisure or everyday journeys. As a first step we built the Bristol and Bath Railway Path, (one of the most popular sections of the whole National Cycle Network), the riverside route to Portishead, and

rebuilt the towpath of the Kennet and Avon Canal all the way from Bath to Devizes. The latter was the start of a most productive partnership with British Waterways and their support for numerous key sections of the Network where there was no alternative but their towpath.

You will find all these seminal routes in this book and many more. These routes were the backbone of the whole 12,000-mile National Cycle Network, and as such they have a particular resonance for me. Here are cycle routes that explore the coastline, national parks and beautiful towns and cities of the South West peninsula. For families there are many leisurely traffic-free stretches to enjoy; local urban routes give quick access to the stunning countryside that is the hinterland of so many of

The Royal Crescent, Bath

Woolacombe beach

Bluebells in the Forest of Dean

Mousehole harbour

the region's towns and cities; and for those who want longer rides you will find the area brimming with opportunities to stretch your legs and travel miles.

Because in the end the South West is a great place to cycle. If you live here you are privileged. If you are a visitor it will reach out to you and leave you with treasured memories of a green countryside and one never too far from the sea. And by cycling you will be that much closer to all that the region has to offer, to its air and its sights, and you will be on your way to travelling more lightly through our challenging times.

John Grimshaw, CBE
Sustrans President

NATIONAL CYCLE NETWORK FACTS & FIGURES

Most of the routes featured here are part of the National Cycle Network. The aim of this book is to enable you to sample some of the highlights of the region on two wheels, but the rides given here are really just a taster as there are more than 12,000 miles (19,300km) of Network throughout the UK to explore. More than three-quarters of us live within just two miles of one of the routes.

Over a million journeys a day are made on the Network; for special trips like days out and holidays, but also for everyday trips like taking people to school, to work, to the shops, to visit each other and to seek out green spaces. Half of these journeys are made on foot and half by bike, with urban traffic-free sections of the Network seeing the most usage.

The National Cycle Network is host to one of the UK's biggest collections of public art. Sculptures, benches, water fountains, viewing points and award-winning bridges enhance its pathways, making Sustrans one of the most prolific commissioners of public art in the UK.

The Network came into being following the award of the first-ever grant from the lottery, through the Millennium Commission, in 1995. Funding for the Network also came from bike retailers and manufacturers through the Bike Hub, as well as local authorities and councils

UK-wide, and Sustrans' many supporters. Over 2,500 volunteer Rangers give their time to Sustrans to assist in the maintenance of the National Cycle Network by adopting sections of route in communities throughout the UK. They remove glass and litter, cut back vegetation and try to ensure routes are well signed.

Developing and maintaining the National Cycle Network is just one of the ways in which Sustrans pursues its vision of a world in which people can choose to travel in ways that benefit their health and the environment.

We hope that you enjoy using this book to explore the paths and cycleways of the National Cycle Network and we would like to thank the many hundreds of organisations who have worked with Sustrans to develop the walking and cycling routes, including every local authority and council in the UK.

MAP LEGEND

----	Traffic Free/On Road route
O	Ride Start or Finish Point
----	National Cycle Network (Traffic Free)
----	National Cycle Network (On Road)

PH	AA recommended pub		Farm or animal centre		Theme park
	Abbey, cathedral or priory		Garden		Tourist Information Centre
	Abbey, cathedral or priory in ruins		Hill-fort		Viewpoint
	Aquarium		Historic house		Visitor or heritage centre
	Aqueduct or viaduct		Industrial attraction		World Heritage Site (UNESCO)
	Arboretum		Marina		Zoo or wildlife collection
X	Battle site		Monument		AA golf course
	Bird Reserve (RSPB)	M	Museum or gallery		Stadium
	Cadw (Welsh Heritage) site		National Nature Reserve: England, Scotland, Wales		Indoor Arena
A	Campsite				Tennis
	Caravan site		Local nature reserve		Horse racing
	Caravan & campsite		National Trust property		Rugby Union
	Castle		National Trust for Scotland property		Football
	Cave		Picnic site		Athletics
	Country park		Roman remains		Motorsports
	English Heritage site		Steam railway		County cricket

National Cycle Network (traffic-free)
National Cycle Network (on-road)
Cycling in South West England rides
3 Ride Numbers

KEY TO LOCATOR MAP

1 Mousehole, Penzance & Hayle	**15** Portishead Lido to Bristol
2 Mineral Tramways	**16** Bristol & Bath Railway Path
3 The Camel Trail	**17** Kennet & Avon Canal
4 Clay Trails	**18** Colliers Way
5 Tarka Trail: North	**19** Chippenham to Calne
6 Tarka Trail: South	**20** Maiden Newton to Dorchester
7 Granite Way	**21** Rodwell Trail
8 Tavistock to Plymouth	**22** Poole to Ringwood
9 Totnes to Ashprington & Buckfastleigh	**23** Poole Bay
10 A Circuit of the Exe Valley	**24** Forest of Dean Circuit
11 Grand Western Canal	**25** Gloucester to Slimbridge WWT
12 Bridgwater to Chard	**26** Stonehouse & Stroud
13 Bridgwater to Glastonbury	**27** Cotswold Water Park to Swindon
14 Strawberry Line	**28** Swindon to Marlborough

CYCLING WITH CHILDREN

Kids love bikes and love to ride. Cycling helps them to grow up fit, healthy and independent, and introduces them to the wider world and the adventure it holds.

TOP TIPS FOR FAMILY BIKE RIDES:

- Take along snacks, drinks and treats to keep their energy and spirit levels up.
- Don't be too ambitious. It's much better that everyone wants to go out again, than all coming home exhausted, tearful and permanently put off cycling.
- Plan your trip around interesting stops and sights along the way. Don't make journey times any longer than children are happy to sit and play at home.
- Even on a fine day, take extra clothes and waterproofs – just in case. Check that trousers and laces can't get caught in the chain when pedalling along.
- Wrap up toddlers. When a young child is on the back of a bike, they won't be generating heat like the person doing all the pedalling!
- Be careful not to pinch their skin when putting their helmet on. It's easily done and often ends in tears. Just place your forefinger between the clip and the chin.
- Ride in a line with the children in the middle of the adults. If there's only one of you, the adult should be at the rear, keeping an eye on all the children in front. Take special care at road junctions.
- Check that children's bikes are ready to ride Do the brakes and gears work? Is the saddle the right height? Are the tyres pumped up?
- Carry some sticking plasters and antiseptic wipes – kids are far more likely to fall off and graze arms, hands or knees.
- Take a camera to record the trip – memories are made of this.

TRANSPORTING YOUNG CHILDREN ON TWO WHEELS

It's now easier than ever for you to ride your bike with young children.

- Child seats: *6 months to five years (one child)*. Once a baby can support its own head (usually at 6-12 months) they can be carried in a child seat. Seats are fitted mainly to the rear of the bike.
- Trailers: *babies to five years (up to two children)*. Young babies can be strapped into their car seat and carried in a trailer, and older children can be strapped in and protected from the wind and rain.
- Tag-along trailer bikes: *approx four to nine years*. Tag-alongs (the back half of a child's bike attached to the back of an adult one) allow a child to be towed while they either add some of their own pedal power or just freewheel and enjoy the ride.
- Tow bar: *approx four to eight years*. A tow bar converts a standard child's bike to a trailer bike by lifting their front wheel from the ground to prevent them from steering while enabling them to pedal independently. When you reach a safe place, the tow bar can be detached and the child's bike freed.

TEACHING YOUR CHILD TO RIDE

There are lots of ways for children to develop and gain cycling confidence before they head out on their own.

- Tricycles or trikes: available for children from ten months to five years old. They have pedals so kids have all the fun of getting around under their own steam.
- Balance bikes: are like normal bikes but without the pedals. This means children learn to balance, steer and gain confidence on two wheels while being able to place their feet firmly and safely on the ground.

- **Training wheels:** stabilisers give support to the rear of the bike and are the easiest way to learn to ride but potentially the slowest.

BUYING THE RIGHT BIKE FOR YOUR CHILD

Every child develops differently and they may be ready to learn to ride between the ages of three and seven. When children do progress to their own bike, emphasising the fun aspect will help them take the tumbles in their stride. Encouragement and praise are important to help them persevere.

Children's bikes generally fall into age categories based on the average size of a child of a specific age. There are no hard and fast rules, as long as your child isn't stretched and can reach the brakes safely and change gear easily. It's important to buy your child a bike that fits them rather than one they can grow into. Ask your local bike shop for advice and take your child along to try out different makes and sizes.

To find a specialist cycle retailer near you visit www.thecyclingexperts.co.uk

HOT TIPS & COOL TRICKS...

WHAT TO WEAR

For most of the rides featured in this book you do not need any special clothing or footwear. Shoes that are suitable for walking are also fine for cycling. Looser-fitting trousers allow your legs to move more freely, while tops with zips let you regulate your temperature. In cold weather, take gloves and a warm hat; it's also a good idea to pack a waterproof. If you are likely to be out at dusk, take a bright reflective top. If you start to cycle regularly, you may want to invest in some specialist equipment for longer rides, especially padded shorts and gloves.

WHAT TO TAKE

For a short ride, the minimum you will need is a pump and a small tool bag with a puncture repair kit, just in case. However, it is worth considering the following: water bottle, spare inner tube, 'multi-tool' (available from cycle shops), lock, money, sunglasses, lightweight waterproof (some pack down as small as a tennis ball), energy bars, map, camera and a spare top in case it cools down or to keep you warm when you stop for refreshments.

HOW TO TAKE IT

Rucksacks are fine for light loads but can make your back hot and sweaty. For heavier loads and for longer or more regular journeys, you are better off with panniers that attach to a bike rack.

BIKE ACCESSORIES

You may also want to invest in a helmet. A helmet will not prevent accidents from happening but can provide protection if you do fall off your bike. They are particularly recommended for young children. Ultimately, wearing a helmet is a question of individual choice and parents need to make that choice for their children.

A bell is a must for considerate cyclists. A friendly tinkle warns that you are approaching, but never assume others can hear you.

LOCKING YOUR BIKE

Unless you are sitting right next to your bike when you stop for refreshments, it is worth locking it, preferably to something immovable like a post, fence or railings (or a bike stand, of course). If nothing else, lock it to a companion's bike. Bike theft is more common in towns and cities, and if you regularly leave your bike on the streets, it is important to invest in a good-quality lock and to lock and leave your bike in a busy, well-lit location.

GETTING TO THE START OF A RIDE

The best rides are often those that you can do right from your doorstep, maximizing time on your bike and reducing travelling time. If you need to travel to the start of the ride, have you thought about catching a train?

FINDING OUT MORE – WWW.SUSTRANS.ORG.UK

Use the Sustrans website to find out where you can cycle to from home or while you are away on holiday, and browse through a whole host of other useful information.
Visit www.sustrans.org.uk

MAKING THE MOST OF YOUR BIKE

Making a few simple adjustments to your bike will make your ride more enjoyable and comfortable:

- **Saddle height:** raise or lower it so that you have good contact with your pedals (to make the most of your leg power) and so that you can always put a reassuring foot on the ground.
- **Saddle position:** getting the saddle in the right place will help you get the most from your pedal power without straining your body.
- **Handlebars:** well positioned handlebars are crucial for your comfort and important for control of your steering and brakes.

...BIKE MAINTENANCE

Like any machine, a bike will work better and last longer if you care for it properly. Get in the habit of checking your bike regularly – simple checks and maintenance can help you have hassle-free riding and avoid repairs.

- **Tools:** there are specialist tools for specific tasks, but all you need to get started are: a pump, an old toothbrush, lubricants and grease, cleaning rags, a puncture repair kit, tyre levers, allen keys, screwdrivers and spanners.

REGULAR CHECKS

- **Every week:** Check tyres, brakes, lights, handlebars and seat are in good order and tightly secured.
- **Every month:** Wipe clean and lubricate chain with chain oil.
  Wipe the dirt from wheels.
  Check tread on tyres.
  Check brake pads.
  Check gear and brake cables and make sure that gears are changing smoothly.
- **Every year:** Take your bike to an experienced mechanic for a thorough service.
- **Tip:** If in doubt, leave it to the professionals. Bike mechanics are much more affordable than car mechanics, and some will even collect the bike from your home and return it to you when all the work is done.

FIXING A PUNCTURE

Punctures don't happen often and are easy to fix yourself. If you don't fancy repairing a puncture on your journey, carry a spare inner tube and a pump so you can change the tube, then fix the puncture when you get home. If you don't mind repairing punctures when they happen, make sure you carry your repair kit and pump with you at all times. All puncture repair kits have full instructions with easy-to-follow pictures.

Alternatively, if you don't want to get your hands dirty, just visit your local bike shop and they will fix the puncture for you.

Regular checks and inspections

Mending a puncture, easy peasy

Yearly professional checks and servicing

MOUSEHOLE, PENZANCE & HAYLE

This is part of the First & Last Trail from Land's End and is an appropriate place to start this guide to routes in the South West. The route includes the picturesque harbour of Mousehole, the fishing port of Newlyn, Penzance, which is the terminus of the railway from London, Mount's Bay's Promenade, and St Michael's Mount.

Just off the shore at Marazion stands St Michael's Mount. This sentinel in the bay was given its name by King Edward the Confessor, after the Norman abbey Mont Saint Michel. Its older Cornish name – 'Karrek Loos y'n Koos', meaning 'grey rock in the wood' – may evoke a time when the mount was connected to the shore as part of the lost lands spoken of in the Legend of the Lyonesse, an ancient kingdom drowned by the sea. Now you can walk out on a granite causeway at low tide or take a ferry in the summer.

St Michael's Mount seen from Marazion

ROUTE INFORMATION

National Cycle Route: 3
Start: Mousehole Harbour.
Finish: Harbour Master's Office, Hayle.
Distance: 13 miles (21km).
Grade: Easy.
Surface: Mostly tarmac.
Hills: Almost level throughout.

YOUNG & INEXPERIENCED CYCLISTS

The route from Mount's Bay is suitable for young and inexperienced cyclists, as most of the on-road sections can be avoided by the careful use of promenade and seaside paths.

REFRESHMENTS

- Old Pilchard Press (cafe), Mousehole.
- Ship Inn, Mousehole.
- Duke Street Cafe, Newlyn.
- Tolcarne Inn, Newlyn.
- Jordan's Cafe and Station House (pub) at the railway bridge west of Marazion.
- Godolphin Arms, Marazion.
- Mad Hatter Tearoom and B&B, and various pubs in Hayle.

THINGS TO SEE & DO

- **Jubilee Pool, Penzance:** Art Deco open-air lido; 01736 369224; www.jubileepool.co.uk
- **St Michael's Mount, Marazion:** medieval castle and church perched on a craggy isle; 01736 710507; www.nationaltrust.org.uk; www.stmichaelsmount.co.uk
- **King George V Memorial Walk, Hayle:** lovely level walk offering views over Copperhouse Pool, an SSSI (Site of Special Scientific Interest); www.cornwall.gov.uk
- **Paradise Park Wildlife Sanctuary, Hayle:** built around a Victorian walled garden, this family attraction features a tropical bird garden, tropical plants and animals, and is home to the World Parrot Trust; 01736 751020; www.paradisepark.org.uk

TRAIN STATIONS

Penzance; St Erth; Hayle.

BIKE HIRE

- **Cycle Centre, Penzance:** 01736 351671; www.cornwallcyclecentre.co.uk
- **Pedals Bike Hire, Penzance:** 01736 360600; www.penzance.co.uk/transport/cycle.htm
- **R.C. Pender and Son, Penzance:** 01736 365366; www.cyclexuk.co.uk

Boats in Mousehole harbour

FURTHER INFORMATION

- To view or print National Cycle Network routes, visit www.sustrans.org.uk
- Maps for this area are available to buy from www.sustransshop.co.uk
- Cornwall Tourist Information: 01872 322900; www.visitcornwall.com
- Penzance Tourist Information: 01736 362207
- Hayle Tourist Information: 01736 754399; www.cyclecornwall.com

ROUTE DESCRIPTION

Leaving Mousehole Harbour, you mostly follow the seaside edge of Cliff Road, past the Penlee Lifeboat Station. Just beyond a line of terrace cottages, turn right and drop down to rock ledges through to Newlyn. You have to use the roads here, and be careful around the Strand, which is really part of the working port. Turn right over Jack Lane Bridge and right again to reach the seafront. You may wish to follow the path along the edge of the sea and green space to reach the shared footway of Western Promenade Road, past Jubilee Pool. After Penzance Dock (for ferries to the Scilly Isles),

you must use the road again before branching right through the car park on a marked lane, towards Penzance train station and the seafront path between the railway and the sea. The seafront path goes around Mount's Bay, leading all the way to the car park by the road to Marazion. Turn right and then left and left again down the old road to Gwallon, which avoids the hill behind Marazion. This ends in a path beside the main road, which you pass under for the quiet road to St Erth (turn left here for the station and local trains to St Ives). Continue north on the road alongside the river for the roadside path into Hayle and the causeway across to St George's Memorial Walk. From here, follow the local road up to the Towans and the beach.

NEARBY CYCLE ROUTES

The ride described above is part of National Route 3, from Penzance to Bristol. Route 3 forms the Cornish Way, a network of routes throughout the county of Cornwall. At Bodmin, it becomes the West Country Way and continues all the way to Bristol.

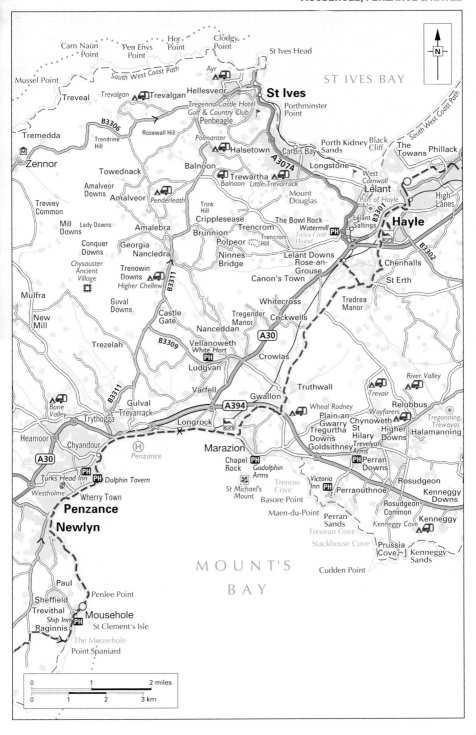

MINERAL TRAMWAYS – MINING TRAILS IN CENTRAL CORNWALL

PORTREATH TO DEVORAN & TRURO

It is difficult to know where to start this ride. You could treat it as a diversion from National Route 3 running through this part of Cornwall, or you could base yourself at Elm Farm Cycle Centre, Cambrose, and spend a while exploring the maze of old trails and railways that thread through this copper and tin mining area, once known as the richest square mile in the old world. Alternatively, you could just ride this Coast to Coast route from the deep blue and exposed Atlantic coast at Portreath Harbour to sheltered Restronguet Creek.

This route mostly follows old railways: Cornwall's earliest, travelling from Portreath to Scorrier, which opened in 1812, and the Redruth & Chasewater Railway, which was the first to use flanged wheels and opened in 1825.

For the return trip you could follow either National Route 3 through Redruth or, much more exciting, the Great Flat Lode Trail (so called because the mineral lode lay at an incline of only 30 degrees, not the usual 70 – the terrain above is hilly, of course!) and the newly opened Portreath Branch Line Trail back to the start. When you have seen the extent of the trails and the numbers of ruined mines, you will not be surprised to learn that an estimated 2 million tonnes of tin was extracted from mines in Devon and Cornwall.

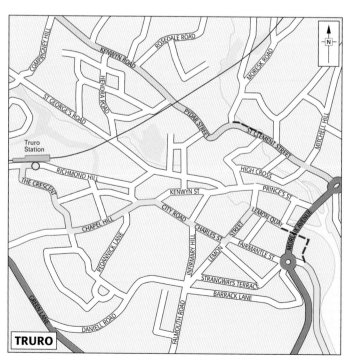

ROUTE INFORMATION

National Routes: 2 and 3 and Mineral Tramways

Start: Portreath Harbour.

Finish: Devoran quayside or Truro.

Distance: To Devoran: 12 miles (19.5km). To Truro: 17 miles (27.5km).

Grade: Easy from Portreath to Devoran, though there are steep hills from Devoran to Truro.

Surface: Mostly gravel.

Hills: Steep hills between Devoran and Truro.

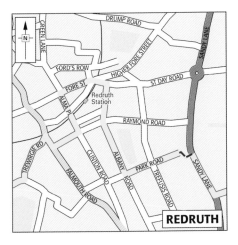

REDRUTH

Old Mine at South Crofty in Cornwall

YOUNG & INEXPERIENCED CYCLISTS

Portreath to Devoran is an excellent starting point for novices and confident children.

REFRESHMENTS

- Lots of choice in Portreath, Redruth and Truro.
- Elm Farm Cycle Centre, Cambrose.
- Fox & Hounds, Scorrier.
- The Old Quay Inn, Devoran.

THINGS TO SEE & DO

- **The Cornwall Centre, Redruth:** for history and documents; 01209 216760; www.cornwall.gov.uk/cornwallcentre
- **Cornish Mines & Engines, Pool:** industrial heritage discovery centre, with two impressive Cornish Beam engines; 01209 713606; www.nationaltrust.org.uk
- **Gwennap Pit:** a depression caused by mining subsidence was turned into an open-air preaching pit; John Wesley, founder of Methodism, preached here some 18 times between 1762 and 1789; 01209 820013; www.cornish-mining.org.uk
- **King Edward Mine Museum, Troon:** oldest complete mine in Cornwall and formerly the training mine for the Camborne School of Mines; 01209 614681;

www.kingedwardmine.co.uk
- **The Shire Horse Farm & Carriage Museum, Treskillard:** large breeds centre with wheelwright's and blacksmith's workshops, and carriage museum; 01209 713606

TRAIN STATIONS

Redruth; Camborne; Perranwell; Truro.

BIKE HIRE

- **Aldridge Cycles, Camborne:** 01209 714970; www.thecyclepeople.com
- **Elm Farm Cycle Centre, Cambrose:** 01209 891498; www.thebikebarn.org
- **Bike Chain Bissoe Bike Hire:** 01872 870341; www.cornwallcyclehire.com

MINERAL TRAMWAYS

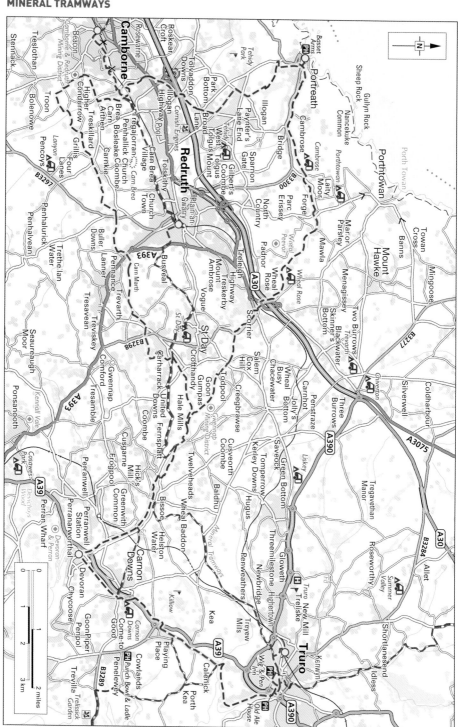

Cycling the Mineral
Tramways route

FURTHER INFORMATION

- To view or print National Cycle Network routes, visit www.sustrans.org.uk
- Maps for this area are available to buy from www.sustransshop.co.uk
- Cornwall Tourist Information: 01872 322900; www.visitcornwall.com
- Truro Tourist Information: 01872 274555; www.truro.gov.uk
- Mineral Tramways Heritage Project: www.cornwall.gov.uk/mineral-tramways

ROUTE DESCRIPTION

Starting from Portreath, the Coast to Coast route is clearly signposted with Engine House symbols. Past Elm Farm Cycle Centre, it runs as a path beside the Tramway Road. At its summit, follow the granite marker stones carefully. The route crosses the A30 on the footway of the Redruth Road, turns right, then crosses left to pass under the mainline railway. Bend around to the left, turn right past the Fox & Hounds pub, and then cross the next road. Go left on its pavement for a bit and then right on a new path to join the railway trail again. You quickly come into the worked-out Poldice Valley. After a couple of desolate miles, turn sharp right at the Millennium Milepost for Bissoe Bike Hire, then follow the river for most

of the rest of the way to the sea. Note that the quays at Devoran are nearly a mile (1.6km) beyond the A39 Falmouth Road Bridge.

Alternatively, to ride to Truro, turn north immediately after passing under the A39 bridge and follow Route 3 up to Carnon Downs.

For the return route, retrace your steps to Twelveheads and then branch left on the Redruth & Chasewater Trail to the Great Flat Lode Trail. In Carharrack, you could turn right following Route 3 past the Gwennap Preaching Pit or, if you have time, go clockwise around the Great Flat Lode. Either way, you can use Route 3 again for Redruth and Camborne stations.

NEARBY CYCLE ROUTES

The ride described above is part of the Mineral Tramways Coast to Coast route, which comprises a sprawling network of trails being developed by the Mineral Tramways Heritage Project. The route from Redruth to Camborne is part of National Route 3, which runs from Bristol to Land's End.

There are also a number of other trails to explore, including the high-level Tresavean Trail, which has spectacular views over the countryside, including the clay tips of St Austell.

THE CAMEL TRAIL – BODMIN TO PADSTOW

Cornwall's spectacular Camel Trail is one of Britain's most popular recreational routes and, along with the Eden Project, a 'must-do' activity for visitors to the county. It runs for 18.5 miles (30km) along the course of the old London & South West Railway, from Wenfordbridge near the foot of Bodmin Moor and the wooded countryside of the upper Camel Valley, down to Bodmin. The town gets its name from the Cornish 'bod meneghi', meaning 'dwelling of the monks' – St Petroc founded a monastery here in the 6th century.

A spur from Bodmin and the line from Wenfordbridge join and continue on to Wadebridge, which has always been an important settlement in north Cornwall, providing the first crossing of the River Camel. It is claimed that large sacks of wool were used to build the foundations of the medieval bridge. From Wadebridge, the trail runs alongside the picturesque Camel estuary as far as Padstow. This section is a paradise for bird-watchers: there are wonderful views of creeks, sandbanks and rocky shores. Wintering wildfowl include wigeons, long-tailed ducks and goldeneyes. Spring and autumn bring many migrants to the estuary, while in summer you will see little egrets, herons, cormorants, oystercatchers and many gulls.

ROUTE INFORMATION
National Routes: 3 and 32
Start: Bodmin Jail (former prison), Bodmin town centre.
Finish: Padstow harbour.
Distance: 12 miles (19.5km).

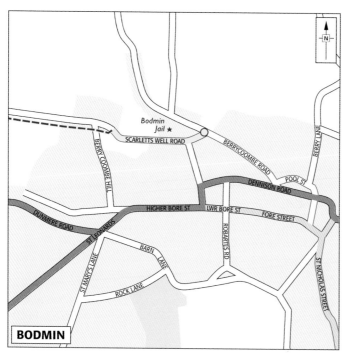

Other options, Wadebridge to Padstow: 6 miles (9.5km); Wenfordbridge to Padstow, via Bodmin (the whole of the Camel Trail): 18.5 miles (30km). You may wish to devise your own lane routes from the ends of the trail back to Bodmin. Be warned – it is hilly around here!
Grade: The Camel Trail itself is easy, running along the course of an old railway line. The link from Bodmin Parkway train station to the start of the trail is fairly strenuous.

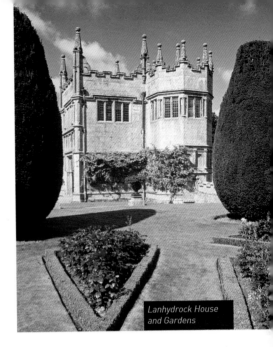

Surface: Variable, mainly gravel surface, suitable for mountain and hybrid bikes.
Hills: The section between Bodmin and Padstow is flat. There is a gentle 61-m (200-ft) climb from Bodmin northeast along the Camel Trail to Wenfordbridge. Between Bodmin Parkway station and the start of the Camel Trail is hilly, with one particularly steep climb.

YOUNG & INEXPERIENCED CYCLISTS
The Camel Trail is ideal for young children, with lots to see along the way. You have to go through the centre of Wadebridge on streets but there are so many cyclists that traffic does not pose the normal threats. The (hilly) route from Bodmin Parkway train station to the Camel Trail is mostly on-road, and includes the Millennium bridge over the A30. Care should be taken crossing the A389 in Bodmin.

Lanhydrock House and Gardens

REFRESHMENTS
- Lots of choice in Bodmin, Wadebridge and Padstow.
- Borough Arms, Dunmere: cycle-friendly pub with direct access from the Trail and a dedicated free car park for Trail users.
- Tea shop near Boscarne Junction.
- Wine tastings at Camel Valley Vineyard.

THINGS TO SEE & DO
Bodmin:
- **Bodmin Jail:** last county jail in Cornwall, eventually closing in 1927; 01208 76292; www.bodminjail.org
- **Bodmin and Wenford Railway:** steam train rides; 0845 125 9678; www.bodminandwenfordrailway.co.uk
- **Bodmin Museum:** 01208 77067; www.bodmin.gov.uk
- **Pencarrow House:** Georgian House with 50 acres of formal and woodland gardens; 01208 841369; www.pencarrow.co.uk
- **Camel Valley Vineyard:** wine tastings; 01208 77959; www.camelvalley.com
- **Lanhydrock House and Gardens:** 01208 265950; www.nationaltrust.org.uk
- **John Betjeman Centre, Wadebridge:** celebration of the life and work of the poet laureate in a restored railway station; 01208 812392; www.johnbetjeman.org.uk

Padstow:
- **National Lobster Hatchery:** 01841 533877; www.nationallobsterhatchery.co.uk
- **Prideaux Place:** Elizabethan manor house; 01841 532411; www.prideauxplace.co.uk

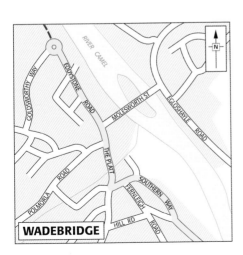

WADEBRIDGE

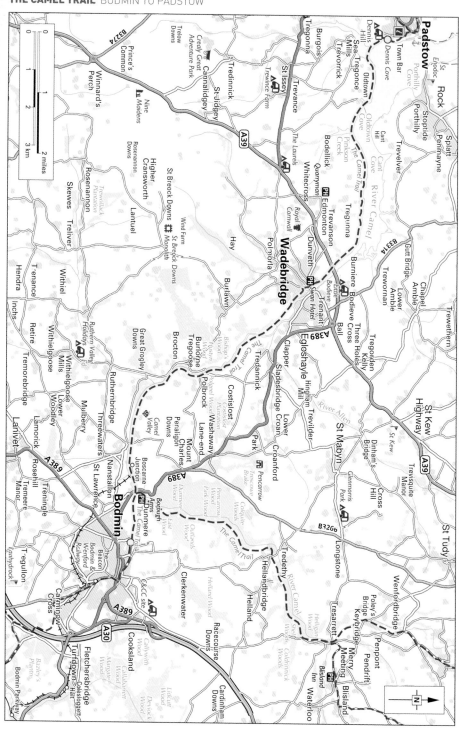

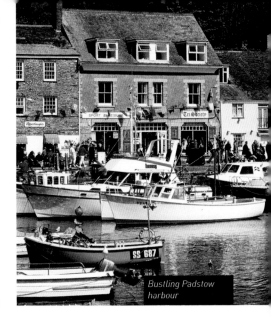
Bustling Padstow harbour

- Rick Stein's Seafood School and restaurants: 01841 532700; www.rickstein.com
- Boat and fishing trips, and ferry to Rock: (carries bicycles)

TRAIN STATIONS
Bodmin Parkway. Bodmin and Boscarne Junction are on the infrequent Bodmin and Wenford tourist line (www.bodminandwenfordrailway.co.uk).

BIKE HIRE
- Bodmin Cycle Hire: 01208 73192; www.bodminbikes.co.uk
- Bridge Bike Hire, Wadebridge: 01208 813050; www.bridgebikehire.co.uk
- Bridge Cycle Hire, Wadebridge: 01208 814545
- Trail Bike Hire, Padstow: 01841 532594; www.trailbikehire.co.uk
- Padstow Cycle Hire: 01841 533533; www.padstowcyclehire.co.uk

FURTHER INFORMATION
- To view or print National Cycle Network routes, visit www.sustrans.org.uk
- Maps for this area are available to buy from www.sustransshop.co.uk
- Dedicated Camel Trail information at www.destination-cornwall.co.uk
- Cornwall Tourist Information: 01208 265632; www.visitnorthcornwall.com

ROUTE DESCRIPTION
From the old jail in Bodmin, follow the Camel Trail along the course of an old railway line, through the wooded valley of the River Camel towards the busy market town of Wadebridge. From Wadebridge, the trail follows the sandy shores of the Camel estuary, with wonderful views of creeks, sandbanks and rocky shores, until the attractive harbour town of Padstow. If you lock your bike in Padstow, you can continue on foot along the coast path to Stepper Point to experience magnificent views. Bikes can be taken on the ferry from Padstow to Rock to explore the lanes to Chapel Amble and on to Wadebridge to complete a circumnavigation of the estuary. In addition to there-and-back rides along the Camel Trail, you could make loops using the network of country lanes, to explore the coastline east of the estuary at Port Isaac, Polzeath and Rock, or west of Bodmin to Ruthernbridge, Rosenannon and beyond.

NEARBY CYCLE ROUTES
The Camel Trail is part of the Cornish Way (National Routes 3 and 32) and the start/finish of the West Country Way (National Route 3), which runs from Padstow to Bristol and Bath.

The Camel Trail links with other options:
- Mountain bikers can access Bishop and Hustyn Woods from the Trail at Polbrock Bridge, 3 miles (5km) from Wadebridge, towards Bodmin (National Route 32).
- Head south from Bodmin to Lanhydrock House, 3 miles (5km), and on to the Eden Project, 8 miles (13km), reached through the idyllic Luxulyan Valley (National Route 3).
- There are forest trails in Cardinham Woods, east of Bodmin, and a signed link from the Camel Trail to the Cornwall Showground, but this involves a strenuous climb.

CLAY TRAILS – MEVAGISSEY TO ST AUSTELL & PAR BEACH

This ride compresses much of Cornwall's landscape and heritage into a single journey. Harbours, beaches, gardens and mines are all tightly packed in, so that when you look down into the emerald blue waters of Lansalson China Clay works, all ringed with rhododendrons, you don't know where industry ends and gardens begin.

The ride starts at the traditional Cornish harbour of Mevagissey, climbs up to The Lost Gardens of Heligan and then drops down the old carriage drive to run alongside the St Austell river. After the town, you follow the old mineral railway, past the ruins of clay dries and even through a settling pond to reach the Mining Museum at the China Clay Country Park, Wheal Martyn. Over the last 250 years, more than 120 million tonnes of clay have been extracted from Cornish mines and sent all over the world for making paper, ceramics, paint, pharmaceuticals and cosmetics. The scale of works is huge, as you will see at the Park, and again as you climb up past the flooded Ruddle Clay pit, to cycle along West Carclaze Mica Dam (each tonne of clay left a tonne of mica and 7 tonnes of sand as spoil) and look down into Great Conclaze works. You can now see over St Austell Bay, with the Eden Project below and, in the distance, Par Harbour, from where much of the china clay is exported, and your final destination, Par Beach.

ROUTE INFORMATION
National Routes: 2 and 3, and the Clay Trails
Start: Mevagissey Harbour.
Finish: Par Beach.

China Clay Mining Museum

Distance: 15 miles (24km).
Grade: Easy from Pentewan Beach to the outskirts of St Austell and after to the Clay Museum, and again from St Blazey to Par Beach. However, the ride to the Eden Project involves some challenging gradients.
Surface: Tarmac and smooth stone, with a few short rough sections on steep slopes.
Hills: A steady climb from St Austell to the China Clay Country Park; for the Eden Project there is a 200-m (656-ft) climb.

YOUNG & INEXPERIENCED CYCLISTS
The sections from Pentewan Beach to the outskirts of St Austell, and from St Blazey to Par Beach, are ideal for children and novices. The railway path from St Austell to the Mining Museum is also suitable.

REFRESHMENTS
- Plenty of choice in Mevagissey and St Austell.
- Tea rooms at The Lost Gardens of Heligan, the Mining Museum, the Eden Project and Par Beach.

Mevagissey harbour

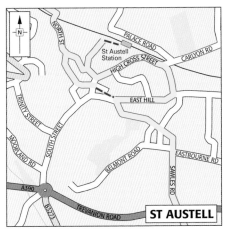

THINGS TO SEE & DO

- **The Lost Gardens of Heligan, Pentewan:** world-renowned restored Victorian gardens and pleasure grounds; includes Wildlife Interpretation Centre; 01726 845100; www.heligan.com
- **China Clay Country Park, Wheal Martyn:** woodland trails and an interactive visitor centre giving an insight into the lives of those who worked in the clay industry; 01726 850362; www.wheal-martyn.com
- **Eden Project, Bodelva:** one of the UK's most popular gardens and conservation tourist attractions, featuring the famous plant biomes and over a million plants, inside and out; 01726 811911; www.edenproject.com

TRAIN STATIONS

St Austell; Par; Bugle.

SAILINGS

Boats, which take cycles, sail in season from Mevagissey to Fowey: 07977 203394 or contact Traveline; 0870 608 2608; www.traveline.co.uk

BIKE HIRE

- Pentewan Valley Cycle Hire, St Austell: 01726 844242; www.pentewanvalleycyclehire.co.uk

FURTHER INFORMATION

- To view or print National Cycle Network routes, visit www.sustrans.org.uk
- Maps for this area are available to buy from www.sustransshop.co.uk
- **St Austell Tourist Information:** 01726 879500; www.visitthecornishriviera.co.uk
- **Cornwall Tourist Information:** 01872 322900; www.visitcornwall.co.uk

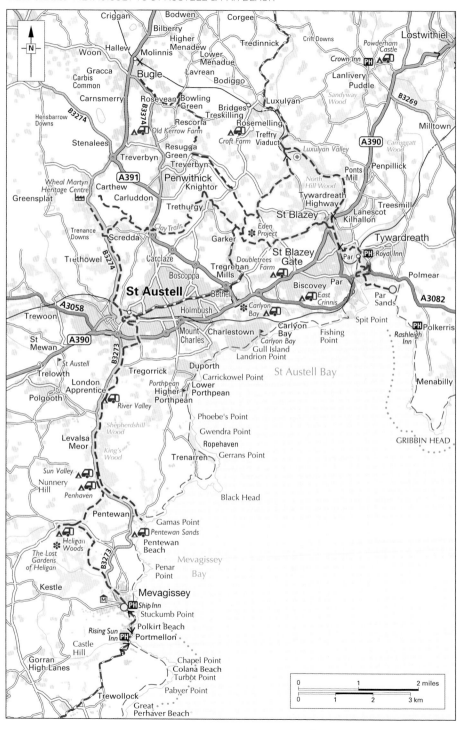

Biomes at the
Eden Project

ROUTE DESCRIPTION

National Route 3 is signposted from Mevagissey
Harbour. Just after crossing the main road,
bear left up a long hillside looking out over the
Lost Gardens of Heligan. At the summit, you
join the old carriage drive. Turn right under the
road bridge for St Austell (for the gardens you
turn left). At the river you have the option of
turning right for Pentewan Beach. Through St
Austell the route climbs steeply up Market Hill.
Turn sharp left past the railway bridge into
Tremena Gardens for the railway path. After
just over a mile (1.6km), fork left over an
award-winning rusting steel bridge for the
Mining Museum or, for the main route, go right
up the hill for Great Carclaze View. Cross the
main road with care and continue on pitside
paths to turn right on the road to Trethurgy.
After a left and right here, turn left after 100m
(110 yards) onto a green lane to the Eden
Project. Here it is best to go through the site
(there is a price reduction for cyclists) and leave
on the path beyond the bus stops down the
valley. Turn left on the road, go up the hill, over
the crossroads and down the long hill past
Cornwood Farm. Turn right in St Blazey, bear
left at the lights and then, almost immediately,
left down a narrow passage to join the Luxulyan
canal path. This leads down to Par station and,

Pond in the Italian
Garden, Heligan

beyond, to Par Beach. If you are taking the
return journey, it is probably best to continue
north along the canal bank, across the main
road beside the railway level crossing and then
continue along a narrow path into the
wonderful Luxulyan Valley. This eventually
brings you out on National Route 3, where you
turn left for Eden again.

NEARBY CYCLE ROUTES

National Route 3 goes to Truro to the west, or
to Lanhydrock House and Bodmin to the east.
The Bugle Clay Trail is being extended from
Bugle station to reach the new Goss Moor
Trails, and will eventually go on to Newquay
and Padstow.

TARKA TRAIL: NORTH – ILFRACOMBE TO BARNSTAPLE

Ilfracombe is the northernmost point of the West Country's premier Devon Coast to Coast cycle route, which runs 102 miles (164km) south to Plymouth. In the summer, you can arrive by boat from Penarth, Clevedon Pier or even, occasionally, from the floating harbour in the centre of Bristol. Express trains used to run nonstop from Waterloo to Ilfracombe, and cyclists can make use of the remains of that track bed to ease some of Devon's hills. But this is not a route to hurry over. The South West Coast Path from Ilfracombe to Woolacombe is well worth the walk, while the west-facing beach at Woolacombe is a mecca for surfing. The route then winds through country lanes to join the long railway path beside the River Taw, ending up at Barnstaple, which is now the terminus for the railway from Exeter.

ROUTE INFORMATION

National Route: 27
Start: Ilfracombe Pier.
Finish: Barnstaple train station.
Distance: 20 miles (32km).
Shorter option; Braunton to Barnstaple town centre: 6 miles (9.5km).
Grade: Mostly easy but the hills (see below) can be strenuous.
Surface: Compacted stone from Ilfracombe to Woolacombe; a gravel track behind Woolacombe Beach; and a tarmac railway path from Braunton to Barnstaple.
Hills: The climb up to Ilfracombe station is fairly strenuous and even the railway path to Turnpike Cross at 201m (660ft) is relentlessly uphill. It is very steep climbing northwards up to Mortehoe and the country lanes can be hilly, as you would expect in Devon.

YOUNG & INEXPERIENCED CYCLISTS

The best section is the 3 miles (5km) downhill from Turnpike Cross back towards Ilfracombe station, while the 5 miles (8km) from Braunton to Barnstaple is particularly memorable if you are sailing along with a westerly wind.

REFRESHMENTS

• Lots of choice in Ilfracombe, Woolacombe, Braunton, and Barnstaple.
• The Red Barn, Woolacombe.

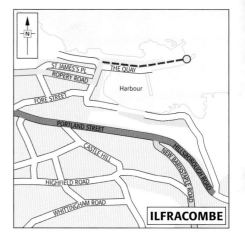

ILFRACOMBE

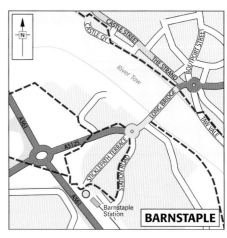

BARNSTAPLE

Woolacombe beach and village

THINGS TO SEE & DO

- **Ilfracombe Beach:** award-winning beach, accessible only through tunnels, hand-carved in the 1820s: 01271 879123; www.tunnelsbeaches.co.uk
- Coastal walk from Ilfracombe to Woolacombe.
- Surfing at Woolacombe Beach: www.iknow-devon.co.uk
- **Braunton Countryside Centre:** free educational centre for planning days out in the area; also holds regular events and talks; 01271 817171; www.brauntoncountrysidecentre.org.uk
- **Barnstaple Pannier Market:** dating back to Saxon times, this popular market, selling fresh produce, crafts and antiques, operates six days a week for most of the year;

Barnstaple town centre is an attractive place to wander around and shop; www.barnstaplepanniermarket.co.uk

TRAIN STATIONS

Barnstaple.

SAILINGS

Passenger sailings from Penarth, Clevedon Pier, and occasionally from the floating harbour in the centre of Bristol to Ilfracombe: 0141 221 8152; www.waverleyexcursions.co.uk

BIKE HIRE

- Otter Cycle Hire, Braunton: 01271 813339
- Biketrail Cycle Shop & Cycle Hire, Fremington: 01271 372586; 07788 133738; www.biketrail.co.uk

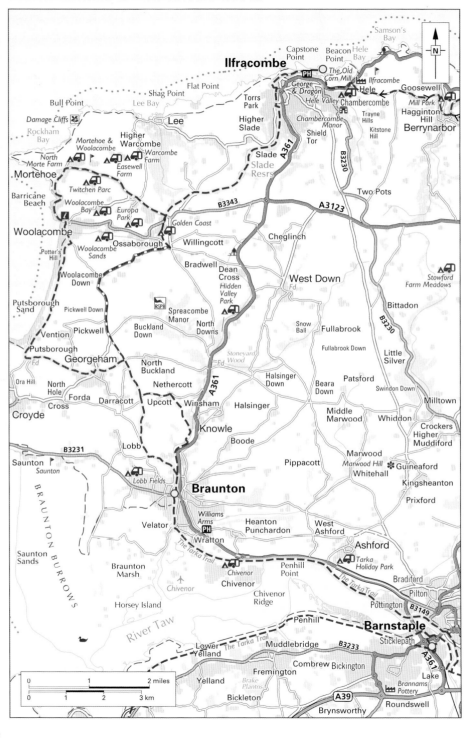

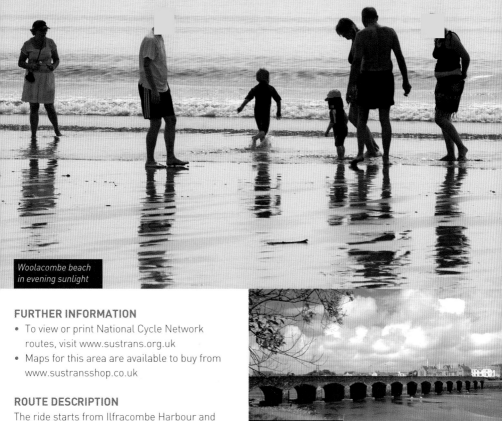

Woolacombe beach in evening sunlight

FURTHER INFORMATION

- To view or print National Cycle Network routes, visit www.sustrans.org.uk
- Maps for this area are available to buy from www.sustransshop.co.uk

ROUTE DESCRIPTION

The ride starts from Ilfracombe Harbour and continues past the shops of the town centre with the conical roofs of the Landmark Theatre on the sea front. Winding through residential streets, Torrs Park and Osbourne Road, you cut through a graveyard to reach Belmont Road, then turn right and left into Station Road to pick up the railway path. This climbs beautifully up the valley past the towns reservoirs, through the tunnel to emerge at Station Road. While the path goes straight on here, turn right and follow the road, which has wide views over the coast before dropping down at Mortehoe to the Esplanade and Woolacombe Beach. Here you have to climb up Challacombe Hill Road a bit before turning right into Marine Drive. At the end of this, follow an almost level bridlepath looking out over the sands to rejoin the lanes at Putsborough. Here, surf fans will want to make a detour to the ever popular Croyde Bay, otherwise cycle on following the lanes to Braunton. Even here you may want to detour to

The 16-arch bridge over the River Taw

take a look at Braunton Great Field, the remains of a medieval strip-farming system, or Chivenor Airbase, before continuing along the railway path to Barnstaple, passing under the new bypass and over a timber swing bridge built with Millennium funding. From the Strand, go straight over the Taw Bridge to the station or follow the riverside path to the old railway bridge and double back past the leisure centre.

NEARBY CYCLE ROUTES

Regional Route 51, along the north Devon coast from Minehead, offers a memorable experience of this coastal fringe of Dartmoor, but it's not for the faint-hearted. National Route 3 runs east from Barnstaple to Tiverton along minor roads and the southern edge of Exmoor, or south to Bideford and Cornwall (see page 36).

TARKA TRAIL: SOUTH – BARNSTAPLE TO GREAT TORRINGTON

The Tarka Line railway, which brought clay from the pits at Meath, survived a little longer than was expected after featuring in the initial cuts set down in the Beeching Report of 1966, and the track was not lifted until 1985. It runs close by the sea with wide views over the estuary all the way to Instow and Bideford before turning south, crossing the river Torridge several times and passing through Landcross Tunnel. Great Torrington is 14 miles (22km) from Barnstaple and you can either stop at the old station, climb the hill to the town centre itself or continue south on the railway path to Meath. This route is exceptionally well connected to public transport, as the railway path starts at Barnstaple station itself where the bike hire centre is also based. Barnstaple is a most attractive town and you may well want to explore this before setting off west.

ROUTE INFORMATION

National Route: 3
Start: Barnstaple train station.
Finish: Great Torrington town centre.
Distance: 16 miles (25.5km).
Grade: Easy.
Surface: Finely packed stone.
Hills: While the railway path itself is to all intents and purposes level, the final climb up to the centre of Great Torrington is severe but then it is only a short walk!

'The Guardian' by Katy Hallett

YOUNG & INEXPERIENCED CYCLISTS

Instow with its beaches across from Appledore or Bideford town centre, or any of the bridges over the Torridge, make for attractive turnaround points for shorter routes.

REFRESHMENTS

- Lots of choice in Barnstaple, Instow, Bideford and Torrington.
- Fremington Quay Cafe.
- Puffing Billy pub at old Torrington station.

THINGS TO SEE & DO

- Barnstaple town centre.
- Beaches at Instow.
- Tarka Cruises, Appledore: one hour passenger ferry trips (May to October); bass and mackerel fishing; 01237 477505; www.appledore-letting.co.uk/Attractions.htm
- Museum of Barnstaple & North Devon: displays covering the natural history and lives of communities in north Devon; 01271 346747; www.devonmuseums.net/barnstaple
- Bideford Railway Heritage Centre: includes the Instow Signal Box, the UK's first listed signal box (open Sundays and bank holidays), and a 1957 railway coach, purchased from the Mid-Hants Railway for use as the Railway Carriage Visitors Centre; www.thenorthdevonfocus.co.uk

Low tide at the estuary at Instow

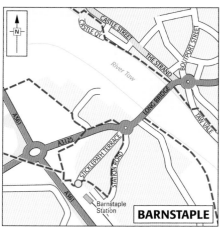

BARNSTAPLE

GREAT TORRINGTON

- Dartington Crystal Factory, Great Torrington: history of Dartington Crystal and live demonstrations of engraving and glass blowing; 01805 626262; www.dartington.co.uk
- Plough Arts Centre, Great Torrington: offers a wide programme of events, including film, theatre and live music; 01805 624624; www.plough-arts.org

TRAIN STATIONS
Barnstaple.

BIKE HIRE
- Tarka Bikes, Barnstaple station: 01271 324202; www.tarkabikes.co.uk
- Bideford Bicycle Hire: 01237 424123; www.bidefordbicyclehire.co.uk
- Torrington Cycle Hire: 01805 622633; www.torringtoncyclehire.co.uk

FURTHER INFORMATION
- To view or print National Cycle Network routes, visit www.sustrans.org.uk
- Maps for this area are available to buy from www.sustransshop.co.uk

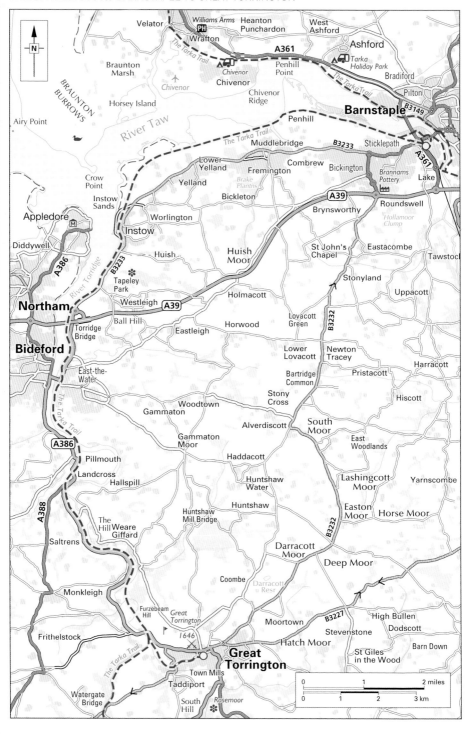

An old signal box on the Tarka Trail

A view of Appledore shoreline at low tide

- Barnstaple Tourist Information:
  01271 375000; www.staynorthdevon.co.uk
- Bideford Tourist Information: 01237 477676
- Torrington Tourist Information:
  01805 624324; www.great-torrington.com

ROUTE DESCRIPTION

Nothing could be easier here, as the path starts from the station entrance, where you can also hire bikes. There is a short tunnel in Instow, where you might prefer to pick up the coastal road for views over the estuary, but otherwise there is not a single diversion from the course of the railway all the way through to Great Torrington. Cross the River Torridge on a fine curved viaduct at Pillmouth and then shortly experience the even temperature of Landcross Tunnel. Just beyond is the turning off to Weare Giffard with its excellent pub. The Tarka Trail then crosses the river again via two viaducts in quick succession before arriving at the former Torrington station. Here you need to continue on the line of the old tramway (don't turn across the river on the railway to Meath). Once you get to Mill Street, you have the choice of going up the hill or going a little further along the old tramway called Rolle Road and picking up one of the diagonal paths leading up to the centre of town. If you want to go to Bideford, leave the railway path at Bideford station and cross the river on the medieval bridge to reach the town centre on the far side.

NEARBY CYCLE ROUTES

This ride forms part of National Route 3, which runs from Bristol to Land's End, and also the Devon Coast to Coast route from Ilfracombe to Plymouth. The Barnstaple and Bideford section of Route 3 is also part of the South West Coast Path. At Great Torrington, you can continue southwards on the Tarka Trail to Meath, where you either branch westwards to Holsworthy and Cornwall or southwards to Okehampton.

GRANITE WAY – OKEHAMPTON TO TAVISTOCK

This third ride on the Devon Coast to Coast route climbs gently to a high point of 290m (950ft) on the western flanks of Dartmoor. The long stretch of railway path offers wonderful views into the heart of the National Park and out over the rolling Devon countryside to the north of Okehampton. Set above the town, Okehampton station is a wonderful time capsule from a bygone age. The ride starts here and runs parallel to the railway line to Meldon quarry, which used to supply the granite ballast stone for railways in southern England, and over the spectacular wrought-iron and steel viaduct at Meldon, the first part of which was built in 1874. The trail then continues along the edge of Dartmoor, where the rocks have eroded into dramatically shaped tors, over Lake Viaduct and on to Lydford, where its castle and gorge are an essential attraction. Minor roads sweep over the moor to Mary Tavy for a final link along the old railway to Tavistock.

ROUTE PLANNER
National Route: 27
Start: Okehampton train station.
Finish: Bedford Square, Tavistock.
Distance: 18 miles (29km).
Grade: Easy, athough there are some hills
Surface: Mostly tarmac.
Hills: Mostly flat on the railway path. Rolling hills and a few steep climbs on linking roads.

YOUNG & INEXPERIENCED CYCLISTS
The route is traffic-free as far as Lake Viaduct. On the road section towards Bridestowe, great care is needed crossing the A386. The lane network through Bridestowe is relatively quiet. The A386 alternative between the end of the railway path and Shortacombe should be attempted only by very experienced cyclists.

REFRESHMENTS
• Lots of choice in Okehampton and Tavistock.
• Tea room at Okehampton station (summer).
• Youth Hostel, Okehampton.
• Highwayman Inn, Sourton: quirky meals and accommodation.
• Bearslake Inn, Lake: also does cream teas.
• Lydford Country House Hotel, Lydford.
• Castle Inn, Lydford.
• Lydford Gorge (National Trust) tea rooms (in season).
• Cafe Liaison, Tavistock.
• Donella's Restaurant: a hidden gem on Paddon's Row, Tavistock.

THINGS TO SEE & DO
• Museum of Dartmoor Life, Okehampton: www.museumofdartmoorlife.eclipse.co.uk
• Okehampton Castle: remains of what was once the largest castle in Devon, dating from the 11th century; www.english-heritage.org.uk
• Dartmoor Railway: 15-mile (24-km) long railway line operating on the route of the old Southern Railway, from Crediton to Okehampton and Meldon Quarry; 01837 55667; www.dartmoorrailway.co.uk
• Sourton Church: built between the 14th and 16th centuries.
• Meldon Viaduct: Victorian wrought- and cast-iron structure from 1874, re-opened in 2002; www.meldonviaduct.co.uk
• Lake Viaduct: built of local stone and offering spectacular views of the Moor; www.meldonviaduct.co.uk
• Lydford Gorge: the deepest gorge in the southwest, with a spectacular 30-m (98-ft) waterfall; reduced entry for those arriving by bike; 01822 820320; www.nationaltrust.org.uk
• Lydford Castle and Saxon Town: 13th-century tower and an earlier Norman earthwork castle; Saxon town defences;

White Lady Falls,
Lydford Gorge

Okehampton town
centre

OKEHAMPTON

Okehampton
Station

www.english-heritage.
org.uk
• Tavistock Pannier
Market: has been held
continuously for over
900 years: 01822
611003; www.
tavistockpannier
market.co.uk
• Canoeing on the
Tamar: trips on the
River Tamar in a
Canadian canoe
between the historic
quays of Morwellham
and Cotehele: 0845
430 1208;
www.canoetamar.
co.uk

TRAIN STATIONS
Okehampton (serviced
by heritage train

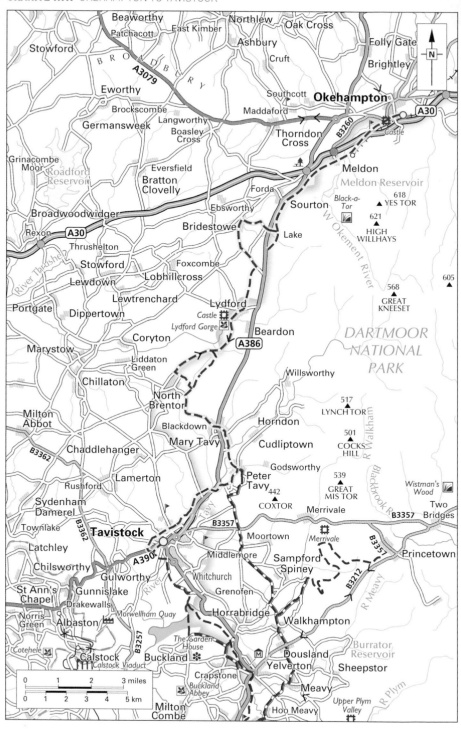

The ruins of
Okehampton Castle

services, which currently run only on certain
weekdays, weekends and bank holidays; a
service from Exeter operates on Sundays
during summer as part of the Dartmoor Sunday
Rover network).

BIKE HIRE
- Tavistock Cycles: 01822 617630;
  www.tavistockcycles.co.uk
- Devon Cycle Hire: 01837 861141;
  www.devoncyclehire.co.uk

FURTHER INFORMATION
- To view or print National Cycle Network
  routes, visit www.sustrans.org.uk
- Maps for this area are available to buy from
  www.sustransshop.co.uk
- Okehampton Tourist Information:
  01837 53020; www.okehamptondevon.co.uk
- Tavistock Tourist Information: 01822 612938

ROUTE DESCRIPTION
Start at Okehampton station and cycle parallel
with the railway to Meldon. Just beyond Lake
Viaduct, turn left and loop under for the Two
Castles Trail Loop via Bridestowe. Alternatively,
if you are a very experienced cyclist, use a
section of the busy A386 to Shortacombe before
turning right to rejoin the railway path. Just

past the entrance to Lydford Gorge, turn left on
a cul-de-sac over the old railway and continue
along the flank of the moors. Beyond Mary Tavy,
you turn down to cross the river on a footbridge
to Peter Tavy and Harford Bridge before picking
up fragments of the railway – this means you
avoid the main road to the site of Tavistock
station, now council offices. For the town
centre, it is best to stay on the old Exeter Road
and drop down the hill to Bedford Square.

NEARBY CYCLE ROUTES
This ride is part of National Route 27, the Devon
Coast to Coast cycle route from Ilfracombe to
Plymouth. North of Okehampton, the route
uses lanes through Hatherleigh and
Sheepwash to reach the Tarka Trail near
Petrockstowe, where it links with National
Route 3, the West Country Way.

Other waymarked or traffic-free rides include:
- The traffic-free Tarka Trail, which starts at
  Meeth, on the A386, about 10 miles (16km)
  north of Okehampton.
- Forest trails in Abbeyford Woods, just north
  of Okehampton.
- The Military Road, south of Okehampton
  Camp, a tough but spectacular 10-mile
  (16-km) loop, mainly roads, into Dartmoor.

TAVISTOCK TO PLYMOUTH

This fourth part of the Devon Coast to Coast route, its southernmost section, is also the most remarkable. Devon County Council and Sustrans have spent over 20 years piecing together a route that threads its way through the foothills of Dartmoor, separate from main roads and smoothing out the gradients. For much of the way, the route runs on the line of Brunel's railway, and you can still see the remains of the masonry piers that carried his five timber viaducts along this route. At Yelverton, the route picks up the original Princetown Tramway, which runs parallel to the even older Drake's Leat, built by that 16th-century buccaneer to bring fresh water to Plymouth. After this you slip down, down the Plym Valley on the old railway line until, at the southern end, you join the line of the Leemoor China Clay Tramway. This runs alongside the remains of the claywork's original narrow canal before finally entering the woods of Saltram House beside the estuary of the River Plym – the Laira. Then, right at the end of the woods, you pick up a remarkable green lane. Perched high on the quarry edge, the lane overlooks Cattewater and Plymouth Sound as you cycle on your way to the Hoe at the centre of Plymouth.

ROUTE INFORMATION
National Route: 27
Start: Bedford Square, Tavistock town.
Finish: The Hoe, Plymouth.
Distance: 19 miles (30.5km).
Grade: Moderate.
Surface: Mostly compacted stone.
Hills: The current route climbs quite steeply out of Tavistock and then drops down to a new temporary crossing of the River Walkham, where it snakes very steeply up again to join the level railway path. There are plans for a new route that will bypass this. There is another hill up to Roborough Down, 120m (394ft) above the centre of Tavistock. From here, it is downhill all the way to Plymouth, with the exception of a small climb at Cattdown.

YOUNG & INEXPERIENCED CYCLISTS
The route is ideal for novices, especially if you don't mind walking a bit. For children, the 6-mile (9.5-km) continuous downhill railway path from Clearbrook is surely the place to convert them to ardent cyclists.

REFRESHMENTS
- Lots of choice in Tavistock and Plymouth.
- Railway Inn, Yelverton.

- Kingstone and Rendezvous Tea Room, Yelverton.
- Skylark Inn, Clearbrook.

THINGS TO SEE & DO
- Site of former RAF Harrowbeer Airfield (1941–49), Yelverton: guided walks available when booked in advance; www.rafharrowbeer.co.uk
- Buckland Abbey, Yelverton: 700-year-old building with fine 16th-century great hall, associated with Elizabethan seafarers Drake and Grenville; 01822 853607; www.nationaltrust.org.uk
- Peregrine Falcon Watch, Cann Viaduct: the Plym Peregrine Project needs volunteers from April to summer to help stop egg collectors; various events are held throughout the year; 01752 341377; www.plym-peregrines.co.uk
- Saltram House: magnificent Georgian house and gardens open to the public; 01752 333500; www.nationaltrust.org.uk
- The National Marine Aquarium, Plymouth: the UK's leading aquarium; includes 50 live exhibits and 3 massive tanks: 01752 220085; www.national-aquarium.co.uk

- Crownhill Fort, Plymouth: 19th-century fort, now a family attraction, with tunnels to explore, real-life cannons, daily gun firing parade and stunning views; 01752 793754; www.crownhillfort.co.uk

TRAIN STATIONS
Plymouth.

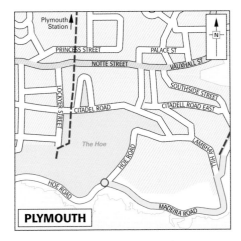

BIKE HIRE
- Tavistock Cycles, Tavistock: 01822 617630; www.tavistockcycles.co.uk
- Dartmoor Cycles, Tavistock: 01822 618178
- Plymouth Cycle Scene, Plymouth: 01752 257701; www.plymouthcyclescene.co.uk

FURTHER INFORMATION
- To view or print National Cycle Network routes, visit www.sustrans.org.uk
- Maps for this area are available to buy from www.sustransshop.co.uk
- Plymouth Tourist Information: 01752 306330; www.visitplymouth.co.uk
- Tavistock Tourist Information: 01822 612938;
- Cycling in Devon: www.devon.gov.uk/cycling
- Devon Tourist Information: 0870 608 5531; www.visitdevon.co.uk

ROUTE DESCRIPTION
Starting from Bedford Square in Tavistock, follow Drake's Walk along the line of the old canal. Cross over the River Tavy to reach Brook Lane. Turn right here and, after half a mile (0.8km), bear left up the hill, past the radio

Smeaton's Tower on Plymouth Hoe

TAVISTOCK TO PLYMOUTH

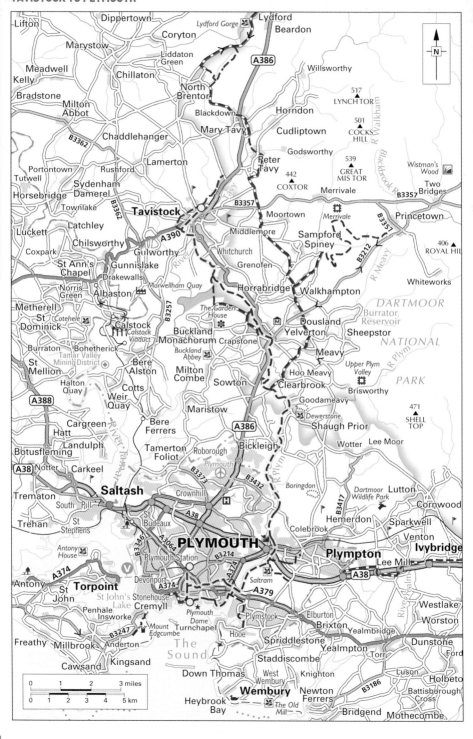

River Tavy, Tavistock

mast towards Grenofen. Just before the village, turn right down a steep hill and, at the riverside bridge, join the new path, which leads you along the river and eventually up to the old railway. Yelverton is a good stopping-off point.

The old railway ran in a tunnel deep beneath the village but we go along the line of the tramway, parallel with the Plymouth Road before veering away over the Common, with magnificent views out over Dartmoor. At Clearbrook Road, go straight across and down to join the railway path, where you will soon go through Goodameavy tunnel. The low-level lighting allows bats to continue to use this tunnel. Ham Viaduct is the first of four magnificent structures all rebuilt in 1890 to replace Brunel's original work, the piers of which you can still see on the east side. The last of the viaducts at Cann Quarry is a convenient place to stop and wander around the riverside, and also to use the telescopes to watch the peregrines, in season, nesting high on the nearby rocks.

At Plym Bridge, the path leaves the railway free for the Plym Valley Railway by joining the adjacent tramway at the bottom of its incline from the Lee Moor China Clay workings. Then it's under the A38 flyovers and over the mainline railway to the tranquillity of the National Trust's Saltram Estate and its woodland path alongside the Laira. At this point, the route divides into two. You can either turn right to go back alongside the river and pick up the city centre from the east, or turn right at the toucan crossing, wind your way though industrial roads until, when you are just about to give up, you come to a short steep hill where a traffic-free lane is perched in a knife-edge of limestone left between two quarries. This takes you magically to the Aquarium, the swing bridge over Sutton Harbour and the walls of the Royal Citadel for your final approach to the Hoe, Smeaton Tower, Drake's Statue and a view over the Sound. If you are going for the Brittany Ferry, carry on around West Hoe Road; if you are catching a train, work your way up through the pedestrianized avenue to the Western Approach Road roundabout subways.

NEARBY CYCLE ROUTES

To the east, National Route 2, the South Coast Route from Dover, is not wholly complete. The best way to pick up the route to Ivybridge, which for the most part runs parallel to the A38, is to go through Saltram House and out through Stag Gates.

TOTNES TO ASHPRINGTON & BUCKFASTLEIGH

Everyone has their own favourite ride and memorable view. The National Cycle Network has many of both, but few can compare with the views down the River Dart from the old drive to Sharpham House. The road was built with the single purpose of providing the visitor with the most romantic and glorious landscape they had ever seen. This alone is excuse enough to introduce you to the green hills of south Devon. Throw in Totnes, Dartington and Buckfastleigh on the edge of Dartmoor, and you will get the idea that this is an unmissable ride where your exertion will be well rewarded!

ROUTE INFORMATION

National Route: 2
Start: Seven Stars Hotel, Totnes.
Finish: Waterman's Arms, Ashprington or Buckfastleigh town centre.

Distance: 2 miles (3km) to Shinner's Bridge.
3 miles (5km) to Ashprington.
8 miles (13km) to Buckfastleigh.
Grade: Mostly easy, though there are some strenuous hills.

Totnes high street is full of character

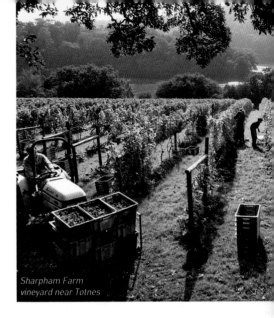

Sharpham Farm vineyard near Totnes

Surface: Tarmac, except for the riverside path, which is smooth stone.

Hills: From Totnes to Shinner's Bridge and Dartington, the route is almost level. The rest is hilly; some sections qualify as strenuous, which means walking for most of us.

YOUNG & INEXPERIENCED CYCLISTS

The route from Totnes to Dartington is perfect for young and inexperienced cyclists. Other sections may need to be walked because of the hills (see above).

REFRESHMENTS

- Lots of choice in Totnes and Buckfastleigh.
- Sharpham Vineyard Cafe, Ashprington.
- The Waterman's Arms, Ashprington
- Crank's Vegetarian Restaurant at the Cider Press Centre, Shinner's Bridge.

THINGS TO SEE & DO

- **Totnes:** a most attractive town, built around the steeply sloping high street, with an Elizabethan market on Tuesdays.
- **St Mary's Church Guild Hall and Norman Castle, Totnes:** 01803 862147; www.devon-online.com/towns/totnes
- **Sharpham House:** the house and its vineyards are perfectly located on a horseshoe loop of the River Dart; 01803 732203; www.sharpham.com
- **Shinner's Bridge, Dartington:** a range of shops selling beautiful arts and crafts.
- **Dartington Hall:** restored medieval hall and gardens, open to visitors and hosting a wide range of concerts and events; 01803 847147; www.dartingtonhall.com
- **Buckfast Abbey, Buckfastleigh:** one of the most visited tourist attractions in Devon, which is still home to a community of Roman Catholic Benedictine monks; guided tours of the abbey; 01364 645504; www.buckfast.org
- **Dartmoor Otters and Buckfast Butterflies, Buckfastleigh:** see otters swim underwater and butterflies emerge in tropical surroundings; 01364 642916; www.ottersandbutterflies.co.uk
- **Buckfastleigh Caves:** this Site of Special Scientific Interest (SSSI) is a complex of caves containing the richest collection of fossil remains of various mammals in Britain; now home to the largest colony of the rare greater horseshoe bat in Britain; their emergence from the caves can be observed at dusk in summer from the church steps in Buckfastleigh; 01626 831006 (Dartmoor rangers); www.dartmoor-npa.gov.uk/la-wowbuckfastleigh
- **Dart Pleasure Boat:** cruise the River Dart, sailing from Totnes to Dartmouth; 01803 834488; www.pdsr.co.uk
- **Steam train ride:** travel through superb scenery, from Kingswear to Paignton; connects with the mainline railways; 01803 834488; www.pdsr.co.uk

TRAIN STATIONS

Totnes.

BIKE HIRE

- **B.R. Trott, Totnes Cycle Hire:** 01803 862493; www.brtrott.co.uk

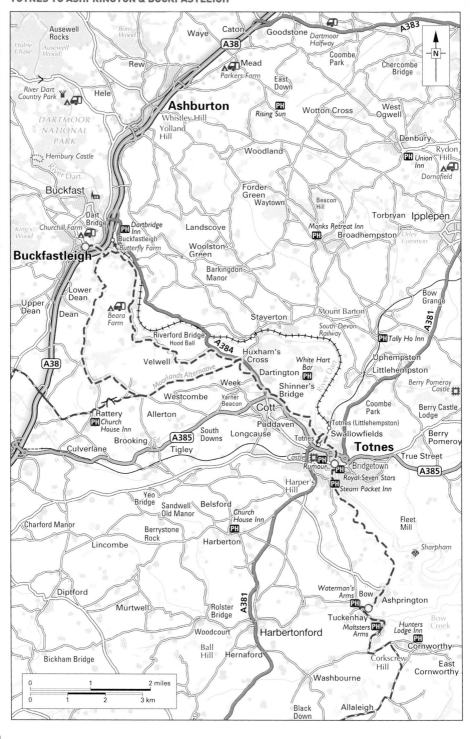

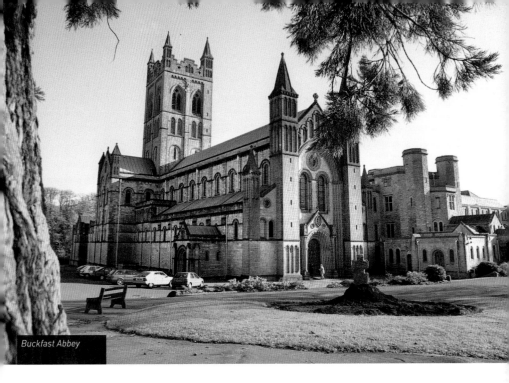
Buckfast Abbey

FURTHER INFORMATION

- To view or print National Cycle Network routes, visit www.sustrans.org.uk
- Maps for this area are available to buy from www.sustransshop.co.uk
- **Totnes Tourist Information:** 01803 863168; www.visitsouthdevon.co.uk

ROUTE DESCRIPTION

Starting outside the Seven Stars Hotel in Totnes, follow the road to Ashprington alongside the river to the boatyard. Turn right up a really steep hill and then, almost immediately, turn left onto the path that leads to the Sharpham Carriage Drive. This is all signposted as National Route 2. The Drive climbs up with views over Totnes for half a mile (0.8km) and then drops in sweeping, voluptuous curves to the riverside. Don't hurry over this section, and if you only use your bike for carrying a picnic to your favourite spot, this is far enough!

Further on, the route diverts from the Drive up a seriously steep hill to reach Ashprington and the rewarding pub, The Waterman's Arms.

Going upstream from Totnes, follow the path beside Morrisons and the sports field to Totnes station, where the route passes under the railway bridge to follow the river to the drive of Dartington Hall. Turn right on the drive and then left along a memorable little path, built by volunteers at a Sustrans summer work camp, straight through to Shinner's Bridge. Dragging yourself away from the path's delights, follow the signposted route beside the main road and then turn left for a magical new path built up to Huxham's Cross. At this point, you have a choice: either turn left and take Route 2 up the hill (in the direction of Plymouth) for a couple of miles and then bear right, following the signs for the local link to Buckfastleigh, or, after 20m (65ft), turn right on a new path to the Steiner School at Hood Manor and an incomplete route to Buckfastleigh. A key section of this route is not yet in place and you must follow narrow Devon lanes, which will challenge you with their contrary hilliness. At Buckfastleigh, pass under the A38 to the town centre or work your way around to the South Devon Railway station, to catch a steam train almost back to the start.

A CIRCUIT OF THE EXE ESTUARY

Since 1995, Exeter has become one of Cycling England's leading Cycling Towns, putting in place a wide range of new routes and cycling programmes. The most ambitious of these is the planned route around the Exe estuary, which will enable people to cycle from the city centre to Topsham and Exmouth, then take the ferry across to Starcross for a return via Turf Lock and its canalside paths. The route described here uses the Topsham ferry to reach the part of the route that is currently open (the Topsham to Exton section is not yet in place). However, by taking a train between Topsham and Exton you can enjoy the complete route to Exmouth and even return to Turf Lock on an interim path along the river bank.

ROUTE INFORMATION
National Route: 2
Start: Exeter St David's train station.
Finish: Exeter St David's train station.
Distance: 12 miles (19.5km).
Grade: Easy.
Surface: Mostly tarmac.
Hills: Almost completely level.

YOUNG & INEXPERIENCED CYCLISTS
Very suitable for young and inexperienced cyclists, with the few road crossings controlled by traffic lights.

REFRESHMENTS
• Lots of choice in Exeter city centre, along the quayside and in Topsham.
• The Turf Hotel, Turf Locks: good views over the estuary and delicious food.

THINGS TO SEE & DO
Exeter
• **Exeter City Centre:** open to cyclists.
• **Exeter Cathedral:** retains its Norman towers but otherwise largely rebuilt by 1400; there is no central tower, which means it has the longest uninterrupted vaulting in England; also an astronomical clock dating back to the 1480s; 01392 285970; www.exeter-cathedral.org.uk

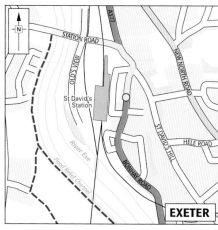

*Exeter Cathedral
north side*

- **Guildhall:** oldest municipal building in
  England still in use; 01392 665500;
  www.exeter.gov.uk
- **Northern Gardens:** laid out by the castle in
  1612 for Exeter residents; now the oldest
  public open space in England.
- **Roman Tunnels:** ancient water tunnels open
  to the public; interpretation centre at Roman
  Gate; 01392 665887;
  www.exetermemories.co.uk

Topsham

- **Topsham Museum:** housed in a late
  17th-century building overlooking the Exe
  estuary in the picturesque village of
  Topsham; includes maritime and wildlife
  exhibits; 01392 873244;
  www.devonmuseums.net/topsham

TRAIN STATIONS

Exeter St David's; Exeter Central; Topsham;
Exton; Lympstone; Exmouth.
  Starcross and Dawlish Warren offer an
occasional service on the south of the estuary.

FERRIES

- Topsham ferry: 07801 203338.
- Starcross ferry: 01626 774770;
  www.exe2sea.co.uk

*Richard Hooker statue,
Exeter Cathedral*

BIKE HIRE

- **Saddles & Paddles, Exeter:** 01392 424241;
  www.saddlepaddle.co.uk
- **Forest Cycle Hire, Exeter:** 01392 833768

FURTHER INFORMATION

- To view or print National Cycle Network

The bridge at Miller's Crossing

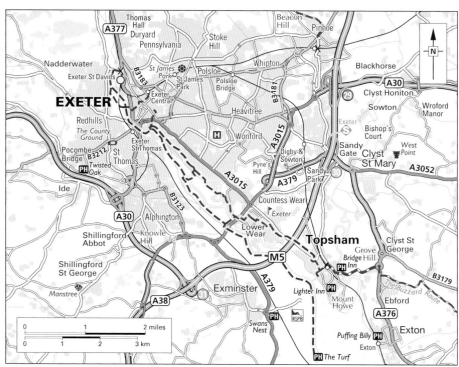

routes, visit www.sustrans.org.uk
- Maps for this area are available to buy from www.sustransshop.co.uk
- **Exeter Tourist Information:** 01392 665700; www.discoverdevon.com
- **Cycling in Devon:** www.devon.gov.uk/cycling
- **Devon Tourist Information:** 0870 608 5531 www.visitdevon.co.uk

ROUTE DESCRIPTION

Starting from the entrance of St David's station, turn left, left again across the level crossing and over the river to the path, going downstream on the far side. Drop down to the riverside promenade, which leads you through to the quayside (cross Miller's Crossing if you want the city centre). Continue along the left-hand side of the river by a series of paths leading through to the youth hostel and bypass. Stay on this side of the river for a generally minor road route, following National Route 2 signs, to Topsham for its ferry over the river. Alternatively, for a longer route, make your way to Topsham and catch the next train to Exton

for the newly built and truly fabulous path to Exmouth, where the Starcross ferry offers yet another way to cross the river, and start the journey back. If you have crossed on the Topsham boat, turn left for the Turf pub at Turf Locks, extensive views over the estuary and maybe a sight of works on the new path to Starcross and bridge over the mainline railway. Return to Exeter along the canal side, following Route 2 signs all the way to the quayside.

NEARBY CYCLE ROUTES

This route is part of National Route 2 from Dover to the Eden Project. The section running east from Exmouth to Budleigh Salterton largely follows an old railway. Haldon Forest on the west of the city is fast becoming a mountain bike centre. You could take the train towards Barnstaple for any number of rides along Devon lanes or to link up with the Tarka Trail to Bideford or Ilfracombe (see rides 5 & 6).

GRAND WESTERN CANAL – TIVERTON PARKWAY TO TAUNTON

This is a good ride with a southwest wind behind you, and an almost perfect station-to-station ride, with regular trains to return you to your starting point if you wish. The ride starts with 5 miles (8km) of the Grand Western Canal, and then follows a necklace of remote country lanes, more or less following the course of the canal, which was never finished but can be explored in places. Eventually, you arrive in Taunton – the county town of Somerset. Although the ride is almost entirely without excitements or highlights, it is always a most satisfying day out on part of the West Country Way, which runs from Bristol to Land's End.

ROUTE INFORMATION
National Route: 3
Start: Tiverton Parkway train station.
Finish: Taunton town centre or train station.
Distance: 20 miles (32km).
Grade: Easy for the canal towpath but moderate as you cycle over the rolling landscape before finally dropping down to Taunton.
Surface: Fine gravel or tarmac.
Hills: Flat on the canal towpath but rolling hills

before you get to Taunton.

YOUNG & INEXPERIENCED CYCLISTS
The canal section is particularly suitable for families.

REFRESHMENTS
- Lots of choice in Tiverton and Taunton.
- Tea rooms in Tiverton Basin.
- The Barge pub in Halberton.
- The Globe Inn in Sampford Peverell.

The Grand Western Canal near Tiverton

THINGS TO SEE & DO
Tiverton
- **Grand Western Canal Country Park**: extends for over 11 miles (17.5km) between Tiverton and Lowdwells; wonderful location for walking, cycling, boating, fishing and picnics; 01884 254072; www.devon.gov.uk/grand_western_canal
- **Tiverton Museum**: over 15 galleries on two floors, showcasing the history of the town; 01884 256295; www.tivertonmuseum.org.uk
- **Cothay Manor**: 15th-century medieval manor house (open by appointment for group visits) with 12 acres of gardens open to the general public; contact for opening times; 01823 672283; www.cothaymanor.co.uk

Taunton
- **Farmers Market**: cheese, meat, bread and vegetables from local producers on sale in the high street every Thursday, from 9 until 3.
- **Steam train ride**: enjoy the age of steam on the West Somerset Railway; 20 miles (32km) of lovely Somerset scenery; 01643 704996; www.west-somerset-railway.co.uk

TRAIN STATIONS
Tiverton Parkway; Taunton

BIKE HIRE
- **Abbotshood Cycle Hire, Halberton**: 01884 820728; www.abbotshoodcyclehire.co.uk
- **King's Cycle Hire, Taunton**: 01823 352272; www.kingscycles.co.uk

FURTHER INFORMATION
- To view or print National Cycle Network routes, visit www.sustrans.org.uk
- Maps for this area are available to buy from www.sustransshop.co.uk
- **Tiverton Tourist Information**: 01884 255827
- **Taunton Tourist Information**: 01823 336344
- **Cycling in Devon**: 01392 383223; www.devon.gov.uk/cycling

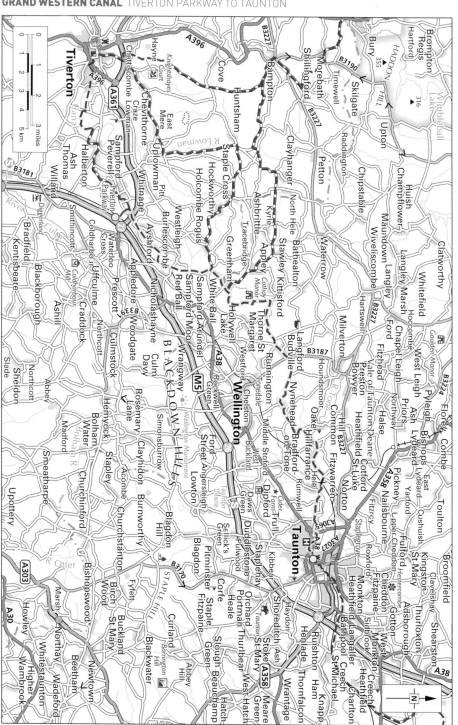

The English Garden
at Cothay Manor

Taunton Vale
farmers market

Along the pretty
Grand Western Canal

ROUTE DESCRIPTION

Leave Tiverton Parkway station by its drive
northwards and cross straight over the main
road at its end to join the canal towpath. Turn
left here if you want Sampford Peverell or
Tiverton itself. Otherwise, turn right and follow
the towpath to its end at Beacon Hill.
Thereafter, it's lanes all the way. The only
villages of any size are Langford Budville,
Nynehead and Hillfarrance – although the last
two are little more than hamlets around a
church, without a pub or refreshments. Before
you embark on the labyrinth of twisting country
lanes, it is worth stopping at Cothay Manor to
see the garden and have refreshments. If, after
this, you get lost or miss the Route 3 signs,
don't panic but do try to keep going in an
easterly direction. Generally, avoid following
signs that point to any significant place, such as
Wellington (unless you want to go there). This is
a route that deliberately bypasses important
places to the extent that the road signs can only
be considered confusing and contrary. When
you reach a level crossing on the way to Upcott,
you are well on the way to Taunton!

NEARBY CYCLE ROUTES

National Route 3 to Tiverton follows the canal
through Sampford Peverell to Halberton, where
you pass through the village on roads, then
rejoin the towpath before linking onto a stretch
of old railway for the town itself.

At Tiverton Parkway station, cross the
footbridge for the path to Willand. Taunton has
some well-established cyclepaths, including
Route 3 on the canal towpath to Bridgwater.

There are a number of attractive circuits you
can do in the area, including:

- At the end of the canal, turn left for
  Holcombe Rogus and follow the Lowman
  Valley Cycle Route towards Tiverton.
- A mile (1.6km) further on from the end of the
  canal, turn left at Greenham for a route on
  country lanes to Bampton (signposted Route
  3 to Exmoor) and another return loop to
  Tiverton, also signposted Route 3.

BRIDGWATER TO CHARD

This ride is an introduction to the Somerset Levels, a watery world where you are never far from rivers or drains, and where Langport, once a port for sea going vessels, is 20 miles (32km) from the sea. It starts at Bridgwater, once a busy port and the terminus of the incomplete canal from Exeter (you can cycle National Route 3 along its towpath to Taunton). The town has an attractive town centre, which is worth exploring. The route takes you to Langport, with its museum of the history of the Levels, past the ruins of Muchelney Abbey and through Kingsbury Episcopi with its Somerset Church tower – a fine example of the passion for ornamental towers built from the good oolite stone and crafted by a few families of stonemasons whose work can be traced to many churches in the area. The route passes by Barrington Court, a National Trust house, with beautiful gardens influenced by Gertrude Jekyll. Then you cycle through the grounds of Dillington Park on your way to Ilminster, which has a magnificent church tower.

At this point, the route joins the line of the old railway and another incomplete canal – from Taunton to Seaton, which would have provided a route from the Bristol Channel to the south coast. This was also the corridor followed by the Taunton Stop Line, a series of well-hidden bunkers, gun emplacements and barricades that were built in 1940 to deter an advancing German army. The route then follows the railway path to Chard, which is the market town for this area.

ROUTE INFORMATION
National Routes: 33 and 339
Start: Fore Street, Bridgwater.
Finish: Guild Hall, Chard.
Distance: 31 miles (50km).
Grade: Easy.
Surface: Mostly tarmac.
Hills: Mostly level with a few gentle hills.

YOUNG & INEXPERIENCED CYCLISTS
While the whole route is suitable for novice cyclists, the Ilminster and Chard sections are particularly suitable for children or learners.

REFRESHMENTS
- Lots of choice in Bridgwater, Langport (Old Wharf Tea Rooms open Sundays) and Ilminster.
- Boat & Anchor, 2 miles (3km) south of Bridgwater on canal side.
- King Alfred Inn, Burrowbridge.
- East Lambrook Manor Gardens tea rooms.
- Barrington Court tea room.

BRIDGWATER

THINGS TO SEE & DO
- **Burrow Mump, Burrowbridge:** solitary natural hillock topped by ruined 14th-century church; nearby Athelney was where Alfred supposedly burnt his cakes before defeating the Vikings; www.isleofavalon.co.uk
- **East Lambrook Manor Gardens:** Grade 1 listed garden; premier example of English

West Quay in
Bridgwater

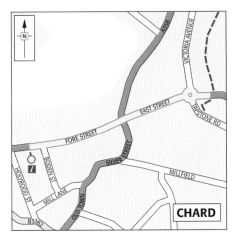

CHARD

Sundial at East
Lambrook Manor

cottage gardening style; 01460 240328;
www.eastlambrook.co.uk
- **Barrington Court:** Tudor manor house
  blending English Gothic and continental
  renaissance architecture; 01460 242614;
  www.nationaltrust.org.uk
- **Taunton Stop Line, near Chard:** section of
  the World War II defensive line, almost 50
  miles (80km) long, designed to prevent the
  invasion of Devon and Cornwall; well worth a
  detour; www.britarch.ac.uk/projects/dob
- **Somerset Cider Brandy Company:** copper
  stills and equipment associated with 150

years of cider making; 01460 240782;
www.ciderbrandy.co.uk

BIKE HIRE
- Langport & River Parrett Visitor Centre &
  Bike Hire: 01458 250350

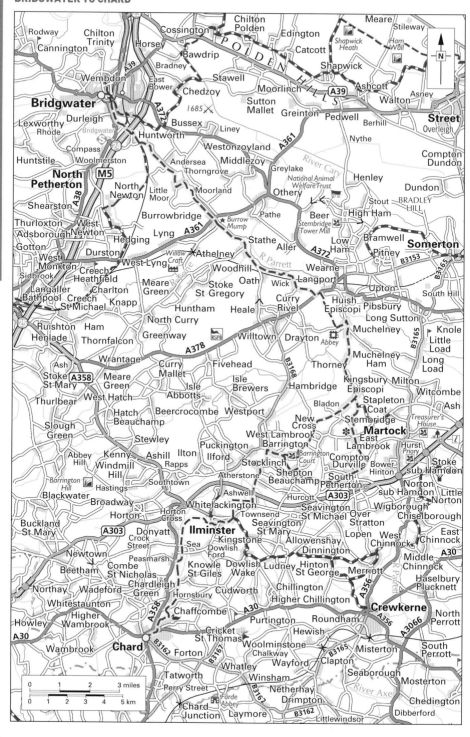

St Michael's church on Burrow Mump

- Ilminster Cycles & Leisure: 01460 52400
- Wheels in Motion, Chard: 01460 63223

FURTHER INFORMATION
- To view or print National Cycle Network routes, visit www.sustrans.org.uk
- Maps for this area are available to buy from www.sustransshop.co.uk
- Bridgwater Tourist Information: 01278 436438; www.visitsomerset.co.uk
- Chard Tourist Information: 01460 65710

ROUTE DESCRIPTION
Starting in the traffic-free centre of Bridgwater, make your way to the riverside and turn south through a small park and under the main road, from where a short length of quiet road leads through to the canal towpath. Alternatively, turn left from the town centre, go along the quayside to the canal basin and follow the canal all the way in a loop around the west side of town. Whichever way you choose, follow the towpath to just past the motorway, cross sides by the Boat & Anchor and leave at the next road bridge – Huntworth Lane. You then follow quiet roads all the way to Langport, always keeping the River Parrett on your left-hand side. There is a short length of main road but, at the bottom of the hill, before Langport, turn right down a

railway path to Muchelney. At Kingsbury Episcopi, either follow the signposted route or bear right for Burrow (perhaps call in at the Somerset Cider Brandy Company) and, just before a steep hill up to Shepton Beauchamp, pick up a farm road to Barrington Court. From here, go south on the road to Whitelackington, but turn sharp right just before the main road for a beautiful ride through the Dillington House Estate. After visiting Ilminster, travel west through a new housing development and join the railway path south to Chard. At the end of Chard Reservoir (built to feed the abandoned canal), turn left on narrow Touches Lane, then right through housing and a park to the bottom of East Street and Fore Street in Chard.

NEARBY CYCLE ROUTES
National Route 3 and 33, Bristol to Taunton, passes through Bridgwater. At Ilminster, the route meets the South Somerset Cycle Route, an excellent route of its kind, 80 miles (129km) long. One option is to follow it past Ham House to Yeovil for a train home. Route 33 is destined to go south to Axminster, where there's also a station, and Seaton on the coast, but it's currently incomplete. Lanes to the west will take you to Axminster, where the route is signposted to the sea.

BRIDGWATER TO GLASTONBURY

This route is pure Somerset, from the muddy tidal river at Bridgwater, across moors, heaths and levels, which are all part of the same watery world a fraction above sea level, to Glastonbury Tor, an isolated pinnacle with far-flung views. It was here that the last Abbot of Glastonbury Abbey, Richard Whiting, was executed in 1539, bringing to an end 1,000 years of monastic life and the destruction of the country's wealthiest monastic house. However, Glastonbury remains a spiritual and mysterious place: the truths and myths of Avalon, of King Arthur and his Queen, and of Joseph of Arimathea's supposed visit, bringing with him a part of the True Cross to flourish as the Thorn of Glastonbury, all make this a site of pilgrimage to this day.

ROUTE INFORMATION

National Route: 3
Start: Fore Street, Bridgwater.
Finish: Glastonbury Tor.
Distance: 19 miles (30.5km).
Grade: Easy.
Surface: Mostly tarmac roads with smooth stone paths between.
Hills: The route is almost level, except for the steep climb up Glastonbury Tor; park your bikes to walk to the summit itself.

YOUNG & INEXPERIENCED CYCLISTS

The Broadway along the Polden Hills is a little busy but, apart from its length, this is a good route for families.

REFRESHMENTS

• Lots of choice in Bridgwater and Glastonbury.
• The Red Tile Country Pub, Cossington.

THINGS TO SEE & DO

• Shapwick Heath Nature Reserve: major wetland nature reserve, important for wintering wildfowl and wading birds; 01458 860120; www.naturalengland.co.uk
• Glastonbury Abbey: once the grandest abbey in England; visitor attractions include costumed guided tours; 36 acres of parkland; 01458 832267; www.glastonburyabbey.com
• Glastonbury Tor: a naturally occurring hill with interesting terracing detail on its slopes; the tower on top, which is all that remains of

a chapel, was originally built in the early 12th century; www.glastonburytor.org.uk
• Somerset Rural Life Museum, Glastonbury: describes the social and domestic life of Victorian Somerset through reconstructed rooms and an exhibition; free entry; 01458 831197; www.somerset.gov.uk

TRAIN STATIONS

Bridgwater.

BIKE HIRE

• Sedgemore Cycles, Bridgwater: 01278 453357; www.sedgemorecycles.co.uk

Kings Drain near Westonzoyland

- Pedalers Cycles, Glastonbury: 01458 834562

FURTHER INFORMATION
- To view or print National Cycle Network routes, visit www.sustrans.org.uk
- Maps for this area are available to buy from www.sustransshop.co.uk
- Bridgwater Tourist Information: 01278 436438; www.visitsomerset.co.uk

- Glastonbury Tourist Information: 01458 832954; www.glastonburytic.co.uk

ROUTE DESCRIPTION
Leave the town centre and cross over the river. Turn right and follow the road beside the River Parrett, across the A39 lights and then bear right onto the riverside path. This passes under the mainline railway and the M5, eventually

BRIDGWATER

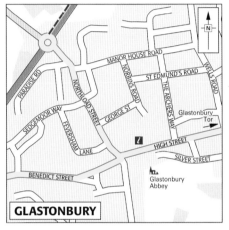

GLASTONBURY

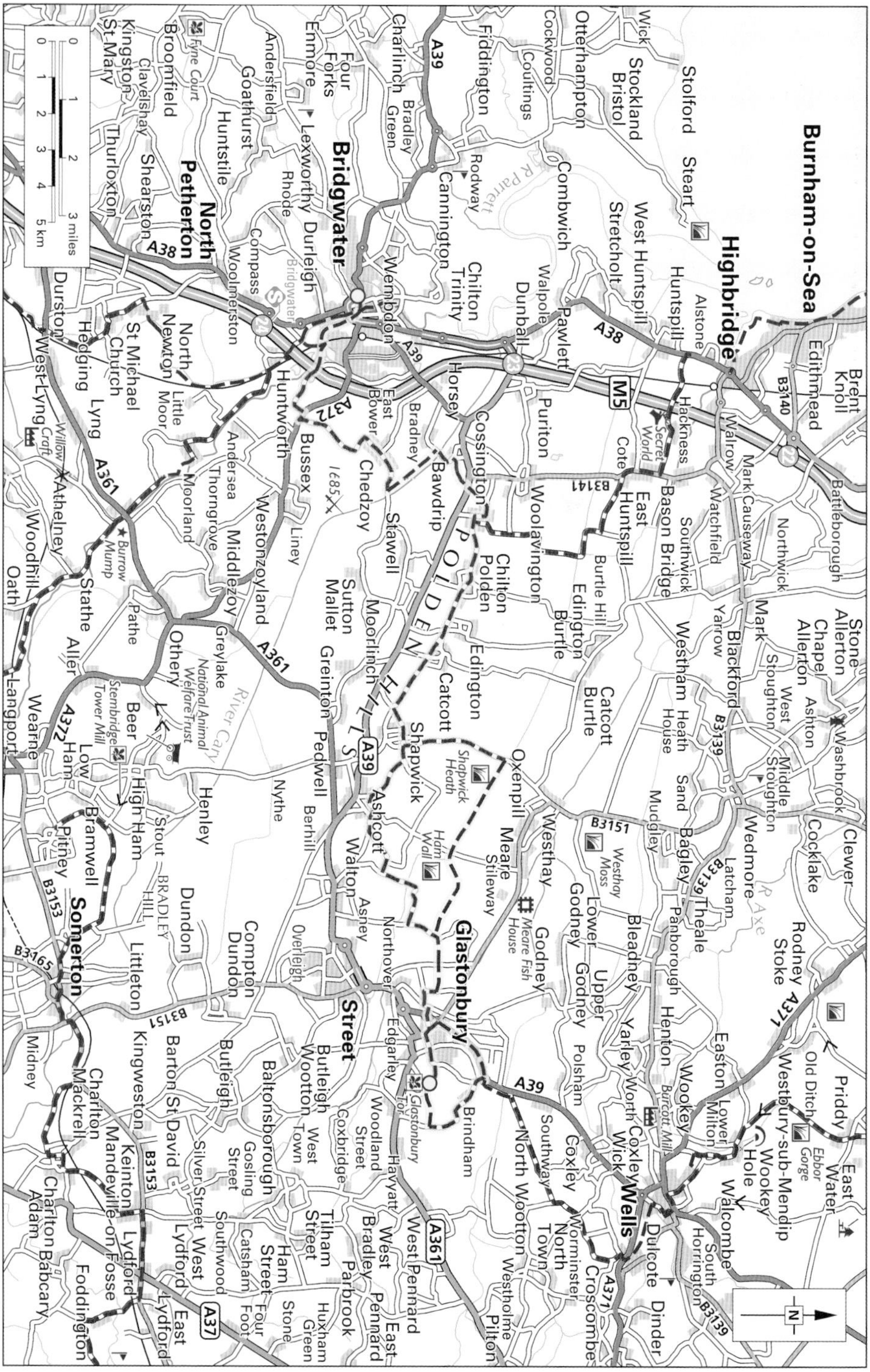
Burnham-on-Sea
Highbridge
Brent Knoll
Edithmead
Stolford
Steart
Wick
Stockland Bristol
Otterhampton
Cockwood
Coultings
Fiddington
Combwich
R Parrett
West Huntspill
Stretcholt
Huntspill
Alstone
Charlinch
Bradley Green
Rodway
Cannington
Chilton Trinity
Walpole
Dunball
Pawlett
Puriton
A39
A38
M5
B3140
B3141
Enmore
Four Forks
Bridgwater
Lexworthy
Durleigh
Rhode
Andersfield
Goathurst
Huntstile
Wembdon
Fyne Court
Broomfield
Kingston St Mary
Clavelshay
Thurloxton
Shearston
North Petherton
Compass
Woolmersdon
North Newton
St Michael Church
Hedging
Durston
West Lyng
Lyng
Little Moor
Huntworth
East Bower
Bradney
Horsey
Cossington
Bawdrip
Chedzoy
Bussex
1685
Andersea
Moorland
Thorngrove
Middlezoy
Westonzoyland
Liney
Stawell
Sutton Mallet
Moorlinch
Chilton Polden
Woolavington
Secret World
Hackness
Cote
East Huntspill
Bason Bridge
Watchfield
Mark Causeway
Walrow
Southwick
Burtle Hill
Edington Burtle
Mark
Yarrow
Northwick
Battleborough
Blackford
Westham
Stone Allerton
Chapel Allerton
Stoughton
West Stoughton
Ashton
Washbrook
Middle Stoughton
Heath House
Sand
Mudgley
Wedmore
Bagley
Cocklake
Clewer
Latcham
Theale
R Axe
Rodney Stoke
Panborough
Willow Craft
Athelney
Burrow Mump
Woodhill
Oath
Stathe
Aller
Pathe
Othery
Greylake
A361
A372
National Animal Welfare Trust
River Cary
POLDEN HILLS
Edington
Catcott
Catcott Burtle
Shapwick
Shapwick Heath
Oxenpill
Westhay
B3151
Westhay Moss
Meare
Stileway
Ham Wall
Greinton
Pedwell
Nythe
Berhill
Ashcott
Walton
Asney
Northover
Glastonbury
Meare Fish House
Godney
Lower Godney
Upper Godney
Bleadney
Henton
Yarley
Polsham
Langport
Wearne
Beer
Stembridge Tower Mill
Low Ham
High Ham
Henley
Stout
BRADLEY HILL
Dundon
Compton Dundon
Overleigh
Street
Bramwell
Pitney
B3153
Somerton
B3165
Littleton
Kingweston
Barton St David
Butleigh
Butleigh Wootton
Baltonsborough
West Town
Coxbridge
Edgarley
Glastonbury Tor
Woodland Street
Brindham
A39
Southway
Coxley
Worth
Burcott Mill
Wookey
Easton
Lower Milton
Old Ditch
Westbury-sub-Mendip
Priddy
A371
Midney
Charlton Mackrell
Keinton Mandeville
Lydford-on-Fosse
Charlton Adam
Charlton Mackrell
Silver Street
Gosling Street
West Lydford
Southwood
Catsham
Four Foot
Ham Street
Stone
Tilham Street
Hayatt
West Bradley
Parbrook
Huxham Green
East Pennard
West Pennard
A361
North Wootton
Westholme
Pilton
Coxley Wick
North Town
Worminster
Croscombe
Wells
Dulcote
Dinder
Wookey Hole
Ebbor Gorge
Walcombe
East Water
South Horrington
B3139
Foddington
East Lydford
Charlton Babcary
A37
N
0 1 2 3 miles
0 1 2 3 4 5 km

*Glastonbury Tor
at sunset*

reaching the country road. Cross right then left over the road to Westonzoyland, and continue to Chedzoy and the King's Sedgemoor Drain. Turn left here onto a riverside path built in three weeks by a Sustrans summer work camp in 2006. This now serves as a route to school in Bawdrip, where you turn right and pick up the railway path bridge under the main road to Glastonbury. At Cossington, follow a parallel minor road along the ridge through a whole string of villages for Shapwick. Either turn right and follow roads via Ashcott or, for a change of pace, turn left and drop down onto the Somerset Levels to join the course of the old railway between Highbridge and Glastonbury. This now makes its way through a landscape of sedge, reed and water, and ends with a willow avenue, planted as a ceremonial approach to Glastonbury itself. Once in the centre of the town you can cycle to the Tor in two ways: either there and back via Bove Lane from the high street, or via a circular route clockwise using the paths alongside the bypass, walking around the foot of the hill to approach the Tor

from the east up Stoke Down Lane. Bikes must be left at the foot of the final approach, where you will find a large carved stone mounted with a small bronze bell. This is the first of nine similar stones marking out the cycling or pilgrimage route from Glastonbury Tor to Wells Cathedral. From the top of the Tor, you can see the whole world from Exmoor to the west, with Hinkley Point power station at the end of the Quantocks beside the silvery Severn estuary, to Pen Pole telecom mast on the Mendips to the east, with Wells tucked in below.

NEARBY CYCLE ROUTES
You can continue along National Route 3 to Wells and Bristol, or from Bridgwater to Taunton along the canal section to Tiverton (which makes for a really special traffic-free route through this watery world), and eventually to Land's End. At Cossington, you can go north to Highbridge and Weston-super-Mare, both of which have stations, along the northern section of the Coast to Coast route from Clevedon to Seaton (Route 31).

STRAWBERRY LINE

The branch line between Yatton and Cheddar was built in 1869 as part of the Great Western Railway and is known as the Strawberry Line because of its delicious cargo from the strawberry fields of Cheddar. The line was well used by passengers and to carry freight until it was closed in 1965, and since then a wealth of wildlife habitats has been allowed to flourish. Volunteers from the Cheddar Valley Railway Walk Society started work on converting the line to a walking and cycling route in 1983 and now it forms a 10-mile (16-km), almost traffic-free route through the picturesque villages of north Somerset.

This ride has no steep gradients and takes in a variety of landscapes, including the flat marshes and cider apple orchards around Yatton, a steep wooded cutting and a tunnel through the Mendips to historic Axbridge, with its picturesque streets. A magnificent perpendicular church and timbered houses surround Axbridge's spacious market square. The route ends in Cheddar, near the foot of spectacular Cheddar Gorge.

ROUTE INFORMATION

National Route: 26
Start: Yatton train station.
Finish: Cheddar town centre.
Distance: 10 miles (16km).
Shorter options, from Yatton to Axbridge:
8 miles (13km); from Axbridge to Cheddar:
2 miles (3km). Longer option to Cheddar Gorge:
11 miles (17.5km)
Grade: Easy.
Surface: Generally firm compacted grit. Some muddy sections near Yatton when wet.
Hills: Short climb approaching Axbridge.

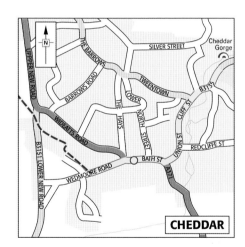

YOUNG & INEXPERIENCED CYCLISTS

The route is mainly traffic-free, although care is needed on crossing and using short sections of busy roads at Congresbury, Sandford and Axbridge, and crossing the A38 after Winscombe.

REFRESHMENTS

- Pubs and cafes in Yatton, Winscombe, Axbridge and Cheddar; also in Congresbury (slightly off-route and care needed on main road into the town).
- Thatchers cider shop and The Railway pub in Sandford.

- Woodborough Arms, Winscombe.
- Good picnic area on Millennium Green, Winscombe.
- The Bank House cafe, Axbridge.
- The White Hart, Cheddar.

THINGS TO SEE & DO

- **Biddle Street:** Site of Special Scientific Interest (SSSI) just outside Yatton, drained by a network of ditches that acts as wet fences between the fields; look out for dragonflies

Inside St John the Baptist church, Axbridge

and reed and sedge warblers;
www.english-nature.org.uk

- **Thatchers cider shop:** try or buy Thatchers cider made in Sandford from local apples; 01934 822862; www.thatcherscider.co.uk
- **Millennium Green, Winscombe:** picnic area converted from the old station, largely by a group of volunteers; includes sculpture crafted from local limestone and a timeline composed of brass plaques along the old platform edge; a May Fair is usually held on the green each year.
- **Axbridge:** picturesque town that has changed little over the centuries; visitors can still wander around the charming medieval streets and soak up hundreds of years of history.
- **King John's Hunting Lodge, Axbridge:** local history museum in a 16th-century wool-merchant's house; 01934 732012; www.nationaltrust.org.uk
- **Cheddar Gorge and Caves:** highest inland cliffs in the country, reaching 152m (500ft); Cheddar Caves were inhabited by our early ancestors 40,000 years ago, and Britain's oldest complete skeleton, Cheddar Man, is on display; 01934 742343; www.cheddarcaves.co.uk

Entrance arch at Yatton Station

TRAIN STATIONS
Yatton.

BIKE HIRE
- **Cheddar Cycle Store:** 01934 741300; www.cheddarcyclestore.co.uk

FURTHER INFORMATION
- To view or print National Cycle Network routes, visit www.sustrans.org.uk
- Maps for this area are available to buy from www.sustransshop.co.uk
- **The Strawberry Line walking and cycling route:** www.thestrawberryline.co.uk
- **Cheddar Tourist Information:** 01934 744071; www.visitsomerset.co.uk

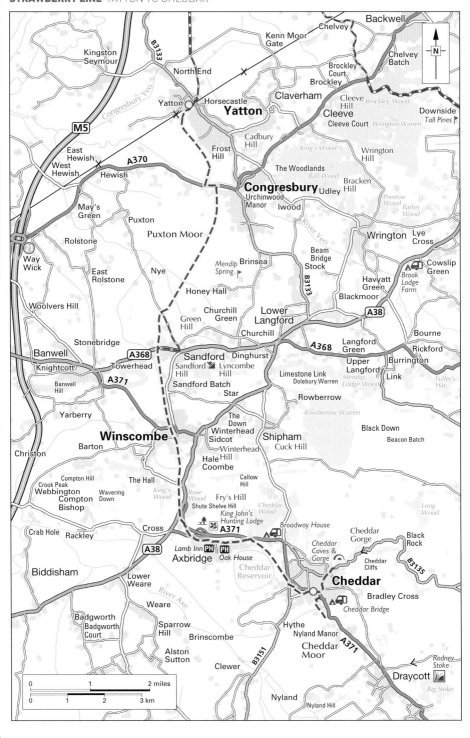

Cheddar Gorge

Gough's Caves,
Cheddar Gorge

ROUTE DESCRIPTION

Exit Yatton train station from Platform 1 and
turn right. At the end of the car park, you will
see the artworks that mark the start of the path
– it's a fairly straightforward route from here.
The track is a little rough and can be muddy but
surface improvements are in the pipeline.

After crossing the River Yeo, the path comes
out onto the main A370 on the approach to
Congresbury and you need to turn left onto the
main road for a few metres before using the
pedestrian crossing to rejoin the traffic-free
route. (For refreshments or toilets, continue on
the main road into Congresbury but be careful,
as there may be fast and heavy traffic.)

Continue through green and leafy woodland
before emerging into the open countryside. You
reach a quiet road taking you into Sandford,
where you turn right onto the A368 for a short
distance. Rejoin the traffic-free path indicated
by the sign just after the pedestrian crossing
lights. A recently opened traffic-free path cuts
out the A368.

After a pleasant stretch, you come to the old
station at Winscombe, with its Millennium
Green. A little further on is Shute Shelve Tunnel
– although there is some lighting to guide you,
you may want to switch on your bike lights.
Soon after, cross the A38 with care. Follow the
signs on the path and then on roads to
Axbridge, and rejoin the path after the town.

The path winds through a housing estate
before ending rather unceremoniously in an
industrial estate. Continue by road into the town
of Cheddar, with its famous Gorge and cave
system, and even more famous cheese!

NEARBY CYCLE ROUTES

National Route 26 continues northwards
towards Clevedon, where it's possible to join
the Avon Cycleway, an 80-mile (129-km) circuit
of the Bristol conurbation that follows quiet
roads and traffic-free paths.

For keen hill climbers, an ascent of Cheddar
Gorge links on quiet roads to National Route 3,
which continues to Bristol on country lanes,
following the River Avon.

PORTISHEAD LIDO TO BRISTOL

This route must have one of the most memorable approaches to any city in the country. Running alongside the Avon Gorge and under Brunel's Clifton Suspension Bridge, it arrives in the city centre via a traffic-free route. It also makes for an excellent there-and-back ride, starting at the community-managed and flourishing open-air swimming pool on the seafront in Portishead. At this point, there is a plaque to mark the closest that any major shipping route comes to the shore in Britain – less than 100m (328ft) off the cliff face. After Pill, you cycle alongside the River Avon. The estuary's colossal tidal range is so great compared with the depth of the river that it appears empty more often than not, simply because all the high water has drained away to the sea. The mud has always coloured the whole Severn estuary brown, and it now travels much further afield through the mud drawings of the Bristol artist Richard Long, who collects his raw material from Sea Mills opposite the riverside path.

Beyond the Clifton Suspension Bridge, the route follows the 'Chocolate Path' beside the Cut, dug by French prisoners of war to bypass the course of the river. This then became the Floating Harbour. When opened in 1809, it was the largest area of water in the world impounded by lock gates. No longer did local vessels have to be built 'shipshape and Bristol fashion' to withstand the twice daily grounding as the docks emptied on the ebb of the tide.

ROUTE INFORMATION
National Routes: 26, 41
Start: Portishead Lido.
Finish: Queen Square, Bristol.
Distance: 12 miles (19.5km).
Grade: Easy.
Surface: Paths through Portishead are compacted stone as is the riverside path.
Hills: Almost none, as this route largely follows the riverside, except for one small climb at Pill.

YOUNG & INEXPERIENCED CYCLISTS
The route is suitable for novices and families.

REFRESHMENTS
• Lots of choice in Portishead and Bristol.
• Me Me Chocolate, Portishead (Marina).
• The Anchor, Pill.
• Avenue Cafe, Queen Square, Bristol.

THINGS TO SEE & DO
• Portishead Lido: newly renovated open-air swimming pool, dating from 1962; 01275 843454

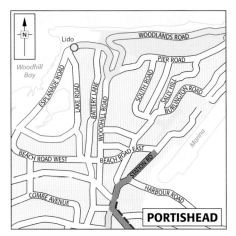

• Battery Point, Portishead: small headland with good views up the Bristol Channel.
• Portishead Marina: interesting development of old docks for housing and boating, with views of the Severn Bridge to the north.
• Lake Grounds, Portishead: model boat sailing.

Clifton Suspension
Bridge

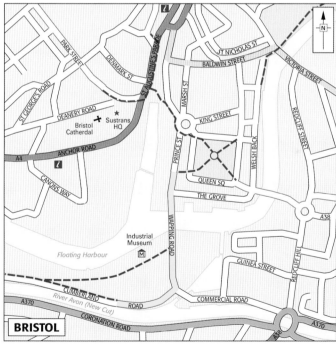

BRISTOL

• SS *Great Britain*,
Bristol: first launched
in 1843 and designed
by Brunel, the ship is
now an award-winning
tourist attraction,
showing life on board
in Victorian times;
0117 926 0680;www.
ssgreatbritain.org

BIKE HIRE
• The Ferry Station,
Narrow Quay, Bristol:
0117 376 3942;
www.ferrystation.co.uk
• Specialized Concept
Store, Bristol: 0117
929 7368

**FURTHER
INFORMATION**
• To view or print
National Cycle
Network routes, visit www.sustrans.org.uk
• Maps for this area are available to buy from
www.sustransshop.co.uk
• Bristol Tourist Information: 0333 321 0101;
www.visitbristol.co.uk

• Clifton Suspension Bridge: Grade I listed
structure designed by Brunel, spanning Avon
Gorge; 0117 974 4664;
www.clifton-suspension-bridge.org.uk

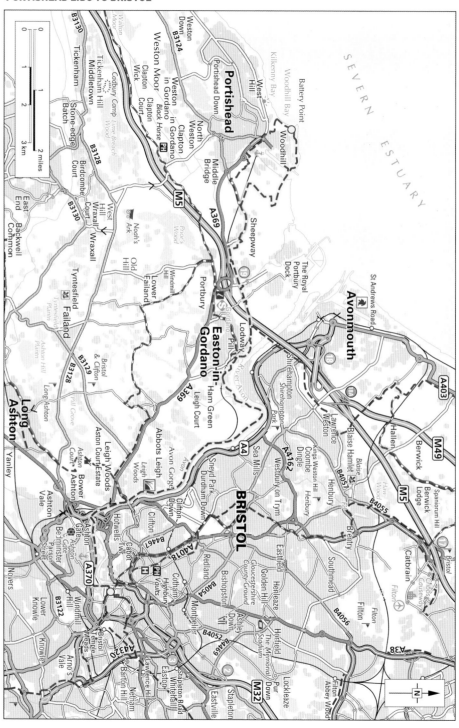

View towards Clifton, beside the Avon

ROUTE DESCRIPTION

Starting from Portishead Lido, turn away up the hill and sharp left through the woods to the Royal Hotel, with a path down to a small beach. From here, walk down the adjacent short flight of steps to the dockside and cross on the lock gate to pick up the developing network of paths being pieced together on the edge of the marshes. Whichever path you take here, you will eventually meet the old main road – the Sheepway. Although this is now bypassed, there is still some traffic. Turn left just before the old railway bridge, to run alongside acres and acres of massed cars (Royal Portbury Dock is Britain's largest importer of cars). At Pill, pass under the viaduct, turn left and left again to go back under the viaduct and then immediately turn right to snake up the hill, through the

grounds of the old Ham Green Isolation hospital, to join the riverside path to Bristol, built by Sustrans in 1980.

Finally, beyond the Suspension Bridge, turn left over the old swing bridge, and right onto the 'Chocolate Path' walk. Just before the slope at its end, either turn left under the main road onto the dockside (beware crane rails and tramlines) or continue along Cumberland Road and turn left into Wapping Road.

NEARBY CYCLE ROUTES

Bristol & Bath National Route 4 to London starts at Queen Square. Route 41 to Gloucester crosses the M5 bridge. At Ashton, there is a link to the new Route 33 to Ashton Court, Nailsea and Cheddar.

BRISTOL & BATH RAILWAY PATH

The Bristol & Bath Railway path was the first major project carried out by Sustrans and now, more than 20 years later, has over a million visits a year. The tarmac path runs from the heart of Bristol to the outskirts of Bath, climbing gently to pass through the tunnel at Staple Hill, skirting the old station at Bitton, with its fine array of steam trains, and crossing the River Avon several times as it approaches Bath. In springtime, the broad-leaved woodland of Kelston Woods is carpeted with bluebells. There are many remarkable sculptures along the way, such as a massive brick fish standing on its head, and a drinking giant.

The cities of Bristol and Bath stand in direct contrast to each other. Bristol is a 'muscular' city, the largest in the west of England, an ancient port built on trade and, latterly, on aerospace industries and financial services. Bath, on the other hand, is an elegant city dating back to Roman times, when it was a prosperous spa known as Aquae Sulis. In building its golden-stoned crescents in the 18th century, the architect John Wood created the prosperous city that 'Beau' Nash made the focus for high society in the Regency era. Today, it is a World Heritage City.

ROUTE INFORMATION
National Route: 4
Start: Castle Park, Bristol, or Bristol Temple Meads train station.
Finish: Bath Abbey.
Distance: 16 miles (26km). Shorter options; from Bristol to Warmley: 6 miles (9.5km); to Bitton: 8.5 miles (13.5km); to Saltford: 11 miles (17.5km).
Grade: Easy.
Surface: Tarmac.
Hills: None.

YOUNG & INEXPERIENCED CYCLISTS
Most of the path is traffic-free and ideal for children and beginners. The signposted approach roads from both Bristol and Bath city centres carry some traffic.

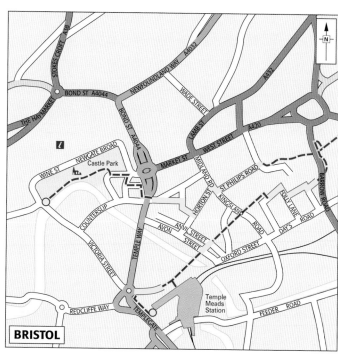

BRISTOL

REFRESHMENTS
• Lots of choice in Bristol.
• Cafes on the railway path at Warmley

The 2000-year old
Roman Baths at Bath

The route is lined
with many sculptures

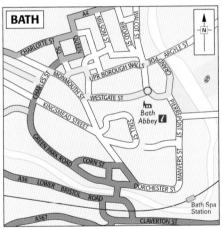

exhibits and activities, including a
planetarium; 0845 345 1235;
www.at-bristol.org.uk

- **Arnolfini and Watershed Art and Media
  Centres:** both situated on the docks, with
  exhibitions, cinema and cafe. Arnolfini: 0117
  917 2300; www.arnolfini.org.uk. Watershed:
  0117 927 5100; www.watershed.co.uk
- **Bristol Museum:** vast permanent collection,
  with changing temporary programmes;
  0117 922 3571; www.bristol.gov.uk
- **Clifton Suspension Bridge:** Grade I listed
  structure spanning Avon Gorge, designed by
  Brunel; 0117 974 4664;
  www.clifton-suspension-bridge.org.uk
- **SS *Great Britain*:** first launched in 1843 and
  built by Brunel, the ship is now an award-
  winning tourist attraction showing life on
  board in Victorian times; 0117 926 0680;
  www.ssgreatbritain.org
- **Bitton station:** steam railway; themed days;
  0117 932 5538; www.avonvalleyrailway.org
- **Artworks en route:** there are a number of
  sculptures between inner Bristol and Bitton.

(seasonal) and Bitton Station (open daily all
year round).
- The Midland Spinner pub, Warmley.
- Bird in Hand and Jolly Sailor pubs (0.5 mile/
  0.8km from path), Saltford.
- Dolphin pub, Locksbrook, Bath.
- Lots of choice in Bath.

THINGS TO SEE & DO
Bristol:
- **Bristol Cathedral:** 0117 926 4879;
  www.bristol-cathedral.co.uk
- **Explore-At-Bristol:** interactive science

Bath:
- **Thermae Bath Spa:** day spa, offering pools
  with natural thermal waters and spa
  treatments; 0844 888 0844;

www.thermaebathspa.com
- **Roman Baths:** magnificent temple and bathing complex, which still flows with natural hot water; 01225 477785; www.romanbaths.co.uk
- **Assembly Rooms:** Georgian public rooms and home to the Fashion Museum; 01225 477173; www.nationaltrust.org.uk
- **Bath Abbey:** founded in 1499 and completed in 1611; 01225 422462; www.bathabbey.org
- **Sally Lunn's House:** the oldest house in Bath and home of the original Bath bun; 01225 461634; www.sallylunns.co.uk
- **No.1 Royal Crescent:** restored Georgian town house; 01225 428126; www.bath-preservation-trust.org.uk

TRAIN STATIONS
Bristol Temple Meads; Bath Spa.

BIKE HIRE
- **Blackboy Cycles, Bristol:** 0117 973 1420; www.blackboycycles.co.uk
- **Webbs of Warmley Cycle Hire:** 0117 967 3676; www.bristolcycles.co.uk
- **Specialized Concept Store, Bristol:** 0117 929 7368; www.specializedconceptstore.co.uk
- **The Ferry Station, Narrow Quay, Bristol:** 0117 376 3942; www.ferrystation.co.uk

FURTHER INFORMATION
- To view or print National Cycle Network routes, visit www.sustrans.org.uk
- Maps for this area are available to buy from www.sustransshop.co.uk
- **Bristol Tourist Information:** 0333 321 0101; www.visitbristol.co.uk
- **Bath Tourist Information:** 0906 711 2000; www.visitbath.co.uk

ROUTE DESCRIPTION
Pick up the route at Castle Park in the centre of Bristol. Alternatively, from Temple Meads train station, cross the new bridge, which is reached via the car park at the rear of the station, into Avon Street. The route then goes through the Dings Home Zone and an industrial area before joining the railway path near Lawrence Hill. From Lawrence Hill, it then loops north towards Fishponds, travelling through east Bristol and continuing through Staple Hill Tunnel, which is lit from 5am to 8.30pm.

The path continues through Mangotsfield, Warmley and Bitton, running parallel for a while with the steam railway line. The final section goes through Saltford before reaching Newbridge, in Bath. A riverside path takes you into the centre of Bath and towards Bath Spa train station. Local cycle routes take you into the city centre.

NEARBY CYCLE ROUTES
National Route 4 runs from South Wales to London and uses the whole of the railway path. Together, National Routes 4 and 41 form the Severn & Thames Cycle Route from Gloucester to Newbury. National Route 3, the West Country Way and the Cornish Way, heads southwest from Bristol all the way to Land's End.

Other waymarked or traffic-free rides include:
- The section of the railway path between Saltford and Mangotsfield, which forms a part of the Avon Cycleway, an 85-mile (137-km) signposted route using the network of quiet lanes around Bristol.
- The 5-mile (8-km), traffic-free Pill Riverside Path, which runs from the Bristol Harbourside along Cumberland Road, then alongside the River Avon to Pill, passing beneath the Clifton Suspension Bridge. There is also a link to this path through Leigh Woods.
- The Kennet & Avon Canal Towpath, a beautiful route from Bath to Devizes via Bradford-on-Avon (see page 78).
- The canal towpath from Bath to Dundas Aqueduct, which joins National Route 24 to Radstock and Frome on the Colliers Way.

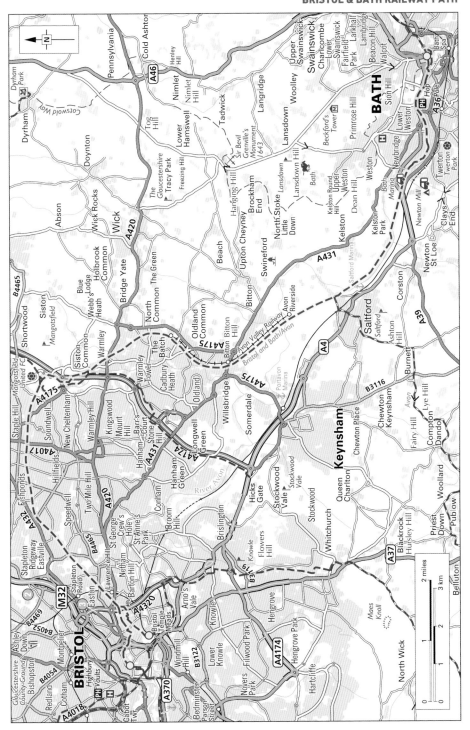

KENNET & AVON CANAL

The best time to follow this route might be in the autumn, when the beech woods at Limpley Stoke are brilliant in the fading sun, or in the springtime, when the hedges are a mass of hawthorn blossom. In summer, on the other hand, you can sit by the river at Claverton Weir, while in winter, this long level route through the Golden Valley is the trip of choice for walkers and cyclists alike. The route follows the towpath of the Kennet and Avon Canal all the way from Bath to Trowbridge. The canal was built by John Rennie and opened in 1810. Its construction was a huge achievement and included a long flight of 29 locks straight up the hillside at Devizes, and two aqueducts over the River Avon. The canal put an end to water shortages at its Savernake summit, and also kept the water in where the rising winter water table in the limestone rocks literally blasted holes upwards through clay puddles!

This canal-side route avoids the main trunk road running through the valley, the old turnpike road to Warminster built in 1800, and it parallels the much more ancient route of the River Avon. It is thought that it was along this route that the blue stones from Preseli may have been rafted to Stonehenge thousands of years ago.

ROUTE INFORMATION

National Route: 4
Start: Bath Abbey.
Finish: Bradford-on-Avon train station or Trowbridge train station.
Distance: To Bradford-on-Avon train station: 9.5 miles (15km); to Trowbridge train station: 13 miles (21km).
Grade: Easy.
Surface: Compacted stone.
Hills: None.

YOUNG & INEXPERIENCED CYCLISTS

This route is very suitable for families and novice cyclists throughout.

REFRESHMENTS

- Lots of choice in Bath and Bradford-on-Avon.
- The George Inn, Bathampton.
- Teashops on the Somerset Coal Canal at Dundas.
- The Angelfish restaurant, Monkton Combe
- Cross Guns pub, Avoncliff.

THINGS TO SEE & DO

- **Thermae Bath Spa:** day spa, offering pools with natural thermal waters and spa

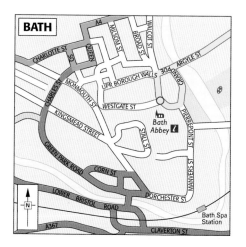

treatments; 0844 888 0844; www.thermaebathspa.com
- **Roman Baths:** magnificent temple and bathing complex, which still flows with naturally hot water; 01225 477785; www.romanbaths.co.uk
- **Assembly Rooms:** Georgian public rooms and home to the Fashion Museum; 01225 477173; www.nationaltrust.org.uk
- **Bath Abbey:** founded in 1499 and completed in 1611; 01225 422462; www.bathabbey.org

Pulteney Bridge was built in the 1770s

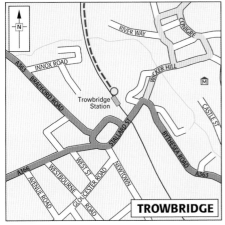

TROWBRIDGE

- **No.1 Royal Crescent**: restored Georgian town house; 01225 428126; www.bath-preservation-trust.org.uk
- **Claverton Pumping Station**: built in 1810 by John Rennie, the station is capable of raising up to 455,000 litres (100,000 gallons) an hour from the River Avon into the Kennet & Avon canal; 01225 483001; www.claverton.org
- **Tithe Barn, Bradford-on-Avon**: early 14th-century barn built as part of the medieval farmstead at Shaftesbury Abbey.
- **Saxon Church, Bradford-on-Avon**: dating from the 10th century but thought to be built

on the foundations of St Aldhelm's church, which dates from the 7th century.

TRAIN STATIONS
Bath Spa; Freshford; Avoncliff; Bradford-on-Avon; Trowbridge.

BIKE HIRE
- Towpath Trail, Bradford-on-Avon: 01225 868068; www.wiltshiretouristguide.com

FURTHER INFORMATION
- To view or print National Cycle Network routes, visit www.sustrans.org.uk
- Maps for this area are available to buy from www.sustransshop.co.uk
- British Waterways: 01452 318000; www.britishwaterways.co.uk
- Bath Tourist Information: 0906 711 2000; www.visitbath.co.uk
- Bradford-on-Avon Tourist Information: 01225 865797; www.bradfordonavon.co.uk
- Trowbridge Tourist Information: 01225 777054; www.trowbridge.gov.uk

ROUTE DESCRIPTION
From Bath Abbey, follow the one-way system to cross the Avon on Pulteney Bridge and continue down the memorable Great Pulteney Street.

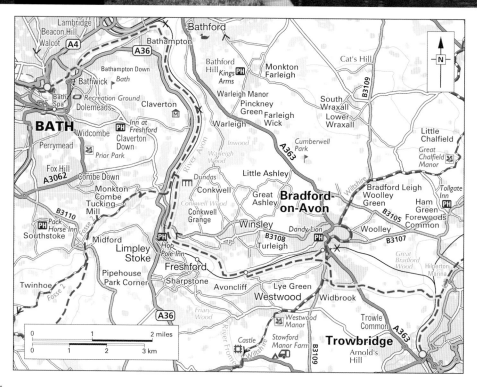

Dundas Aqueduct,
Kennet & Avon Canal

Cycling along the canalside route

The Tithe Barn at Bradford-on-Avon

The route is signposted along the main road but Sydney Gardens behind the Holbein Museum leads onto the canal and gives you the excitement of going through the Beckford Road Tunnel. The canal can be crowded with walkers as well as cyclists, so please be courteous and give way whenever you can.

At Dundas, cross over the canal before the aqueduct to pick up the towpath, which now runs on the right-hand side of the water. Take a moment to walk down the steps on the far side of the aqueduct so that you can admire its achievement of crossing the Avon so boldly. Three miles (5km) further on, you spiral under the far side of Avoncliff Aqueduct to return to the left-hand side of the canal, which you follow all the way to Trowbridge. For Bradford-on-Avon, turn left at the site of the swing bridge and, at the first opportunity, bear left again to pass under the railway to reach the station and town centre. Bradford-on-Avon is notable in hard-core cycling circles for the home and workshop of Alex Moulton, who completely revolutionized bike design with his series of

small-wheeled beauties.

A little further along the towpath, the bulk of the medieval Tithe Barn comes into view, which you simply must stop to see inside – it's free! Cross the road at Bradford Lock, and then, 4 miles (6.5km) further on, turn right over the canal to follow the mainline railway back to Trowbridge station.

NEARBY CYCLE ROUTES

National Route 26 to Midford, Radstock, Frome and Salisbury turns off the Kennet & Avon canal at Dundas Aqueduct, and proceeds along the line of the former Somerset Coal Canal.

At Bradford-on-Avon, you can either join the Wiltshire Cycle Way for Chippenham, or work your way through to Farleigh Hungerford Castle.

At Trowbridge, Route 4 continues along the towpath to Devizes.

COLLIERS WAY – FROME TO RADSTOCK & DUNDAS AQUEDUCT

This ride takes you through the heart of the old Somerset Coal Field, now long closed and grassed over but leaving a heritage of abandoned canals, tramways and railways around which this route is fashioned. In its heyday, Frome was a major woollen town and, indeed, its carpet business has only closed relatively recently. Along the way to Mells, Fussell's Ironworks was one of the country's foremost producers of sharp agricultural implements in the 19th century. You then pass the remains of the canal that James Fussell promoted but never completed, en route to Radstock. The town was the focus of coal mining, and no less than four railways converged there, including the famous Pines Express, which ran from Birmingham to Bournemouth along the course of the Somerset & Dorset Railway.

The section beyond Radstock follows parts of the Somerset & Dorset line, which was built on the course of the former coal tramway. The tramway had, in turn, replaced the coal canal that connected with the Kennet & Avon at Dundas Aqueduct. This canal was surveyed by William Smith, whose house you pass beyond Midford at Tucking Mill. His work in the local coal mines and on this canal construction led him to an understanding of English geology and eventually the preparation of the world's first national geological map. His achievement is commemorated with a column of stone standing on the line of the canal on the way to Midford.

The viaduct at Midford passes over the remains of the tramway incline to Radstock, the Somerset Coal Railway, which featured in the 1953 film *The Titfield Thunderbolt*, the main branch of the Somerset Coal Canal, whose towpath you can follow on foot, and, of course, the main road to Bath. What a concentration of passage in such a rural spot!

Finally, at Monkton Combe, the route rejoins the railway, passing under the Limpley Stoke Viaduct. This was built by the Black Dog Turnpike Trust, run by the McAdam family, and was the last turnpike road built in Britain before the emerging railways replaced stagecoaches. The route then joins the Kennet and Avon Canal, whose fortunes also withered in the face of the much faster competition.

'Simplicity Bench' on the Colliers Way

ROUTE INFORMATION

National Route: 24
Start: Market Place, Frome.
Finish: Dundas Aqueduct, on Kennet & Avon Canal.
Distance: 18 miles (29km).
Shorter option, from Great Elm to Radstock: 5.5 miles (9km).
Grade: Mostly easy but with some steep hills (see Hills below).
Surface: Mostly tarmac, except on the Wellow to Midford path, which is gravel.

The pit wheel at Radstock Museum

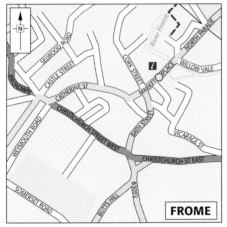

FROME

Hills: Some steep hills at Frome, Great Elm and Shoscombe.

YOUNG & INEXPERIENCED CYCLISTS

The railway path from Great Elm to Radstock is ideal for novices and young children, as is the section from Radstock to Shoscombe and from Wellow to Midford.

REFRESHMENTS

- Lots of choice in Frome.
- Tea & Trade Fairtrade cafe, Radstock.
- Cafe at Dundas Aqueduct.

- Pubs in Wellow, Midford and Monkton Combe.

THINGS TO SEE & DO

- **Somerset & Dorset Railway Heritage Trust, Midsomer Norton:** restored station buildings, steam and diesel locomotives and other rolling stock; cafe, gift shop and second-hand book shop; 01761 411221; www.sdjr.co.uk
- **Vobster Quay Inland Diving, Mells:** diving lessons for beginners and experienced divers; 01373 814666; www.vobster.com
- **Radstock Museum:** exhibitions detailing the coalfield heritage of the area; 01761 437722; www.radstockmuseum.co.uk
- **Somerset Lavender Farm, Faulkland:** wander through lavender fields and visit the healing garden; cafe; seasonal opening (contact for times); 01373 834893; www.somersetlavender.com
- **Wellow Trekking Centre, Wellow:** horse riding, clay pigeon shooting, archery and more; 01225 834376; www.wellowtrekking.com

TRAIN STATIONS

Frome.

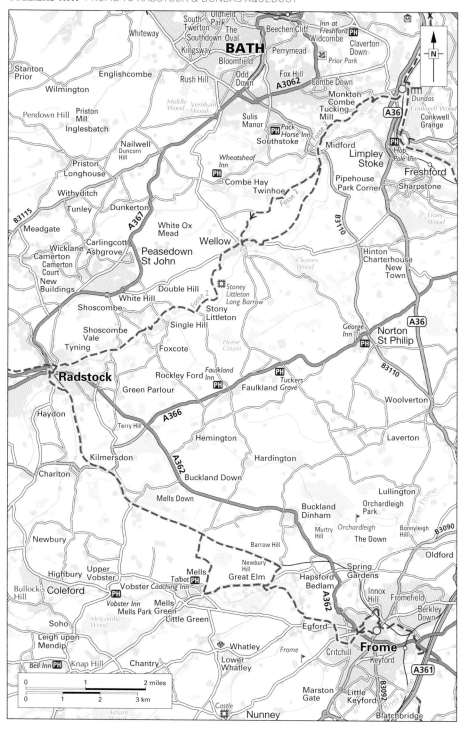

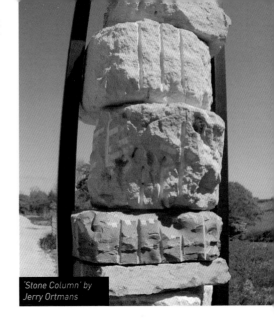

'Stone Column' by
Jerry Ortmans

BIKE HIRE
- Bath & Dundas Canal Co Bike Hire:
  01225 722292; www.bathcanal.com

FURTHER INFORMATION
- To view or print National Cycle Network
  routes, visit www.sustrans.org.uk
- Maps for this area are available to buy from
  www.sustransshop.co.uk
- Colliers Way recreational path:
  www.colliersway.co.uk

ROUTE DESCRIPTION
From the market place in Frome, it is best to
walk up Catherine Street to pick up signposted
roads to Great Elm for the railway path to
Radstock. From here, follow Waterloo Road to
join more sections of railway path through to
Shoscombe Vale, then a quiet road to Wellow
and the railway path to Midford (note that this is
occasionally closed during the shooting
season). The route ends at Dundas Aqueduct.

NEARBY CYCLE ROUTES
At Dundas Aqueduct, this route joins National
Route 4, which runs from Bristol to London.
On Route 4 at Kilmersdon, you can join minor
roads that will become Route 48 to Shepton
Mallet, while, at Frome, Route 24 continues to
Longleat, Salisbury and towards Poole.

Dundas aqueduct, built
by John Rennie in 1804

CHIPPENHAM TO CALNE

Chippenham makes a very good start for a memorable pair of routes in Wiltshire. It's an attractive town with plenty of cafés and an attractive riverside park from which to start your journey. North Wiltshire Council built three magnificent bridges, two over the River Avon here in Chippenham and one over the A4 at Black Dog near Bowood House, in order to make this route possible.

The route to Calne follows the line of the old railway, including sections through attractive woods and looking over the valley of the River Marden. Calne was a coaching town at the foot of the North Wessex Downs, from where you can explore a number of interesting tracks and routes leading across to Silbury Hill, Avebury Stone Circle and Devizes.

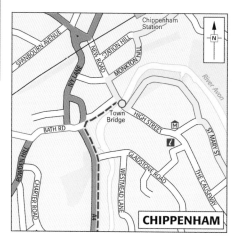

The Orangery at Bowood House

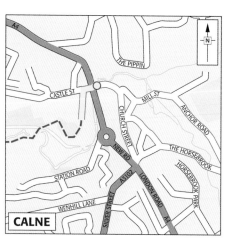

ROUTE INFORMATION

National Route: 403
Start: Town Bridge, Chippenham.
Finish: Steel Head sculpture, Calne.
Distance: Chippenham to Calne: 7 miles
(11km).
Grade: Easy.
Surface: Generally good compacted stone.
Hills: No significant hills.

YOUNG & INEXPERIENCED CYCLISTS

The routes are largely traffic-free and very
suitable for novices and children.

'The Calne Head' by Rick Kirby

REFRESHMENTS

- Lots of choice in Chippenham
  and Calne.

THINGS TO SEE & DO

- **Luckington Court, Chippenham:** location for
  some of the scenes in the 1995 BBC

adaptation of *Pride and Prejudice*; 01666 840488; www.luckingtoncourt.co.uk
- Chippenham Museum & Heritage Centre: variety of exhibitions on the heritage of Chippenham; 01249 705020; www.chippenham.gov.uk
- Bowood Estate, Calne: stately home and gardens covering over 2,000 acres, with hotel, golf course and adventure playground; 01249 812102; www.bowood-estate.co.uk

TRAIN STATIONS
Chippenham.

BIKE HIRE
- Enquire locally.

FURTHER INFORMATION
- To view or print National Cycle Network routes, visit www.sustrans.org.uk

- Maps for this area are available to buy from www.sustransshop.co.uk
- Chippenham Tourist Information: 01249 665970; www.visitwiltshire.co.uk

ROUTE DESCRIPTION
Travel along High Street and turn left at the fine church, continue along St Mary's Street to its end, where you turn left and cross the river on the blue bridge. Follow the path around the fields and climb up to join the railway line at Black Bridge. You are now on the North Wiltshire Rivers Route, the old railway line to Calne. You join a short length of road and cross the line of the old canal at Studley Bridge before rejoining the railway through the site of the long disappeared Stanley Abbey, which you can see on either side as a series of mounds and ditches. If you want to visit Bowood House, continue on the road to Studley, turn right in

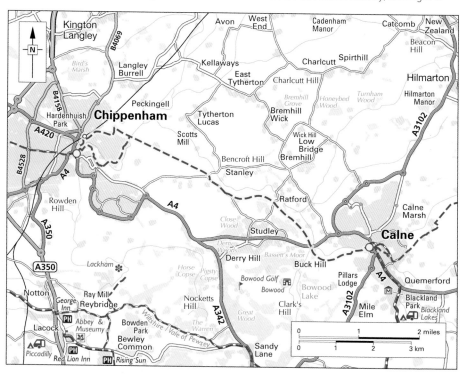

the village and go straight over the A4 for the main drive to the house. Continue cycling on the railway path over the very fine Black Dog Bridge crossing the A4. On your final approach to Calne, drop steeply down into the meadows, cross the canal again and turn right around the castle mound. Continue through the housing development to the town centre, opposite the Steel Head sculpture.

NEARBY CYCLE ROUTES

National Route 4 continues from Calne to Avebury and London. From Calne the Wiltshire Cycleway goes south via Stockley and then north east via the Vale of Pewsey to Lacock where you can visit Lacock Abbey , with its newly restored botanic garden and greenhouse, and the Fox Talbot Museum which celebrates the life and work on William Henry Fox Talbot. Do bear in mind that there are considerable

Baydons Lane Bridge

hills on the Wiltshire Cycle route.

From Lacock follow the Route 4 signs south to Melksham, where you join the Kennet & Avon Canal route for Devizes or Bath.

Lacock Abbey

MAIDEN NEWTON TO DORCHESTER & MAIDEN CASTLE

This Dorset route meanders predominantly along the River Frome, taking you through a number of west Dorset villages on a mix of country lanes, off-road sections, trunk road pavement, and into Dorchester town. Dorchester was founded by the Romans and is now the County Town of Dorset. The off-road section between Cruxton and Southover may not be suitable for touring bikes in winter. Work is ongoing to reduce the number of gates.

After Dorchester, you finish at Maiden Castle, the largest and most complex Iron Age hillfort in Britain, which dates back to 600 BC and is the size of five football pitches. It is worth allowing time to explore its complex defences of massive ditches and banks, which, despite their scale, proved no defence against the Romans, who stormed the site in AD 43.

ROUTE INFORMATION

National Route: 2 and 26
Start: Maiden Newton train station.
Finish: Maiden Castle, via Dorchester.
Distance: 11 miles (18km).
Grade: Moderate.
Surface: Mostly tarmac road or pavement with crushed stone/gravel track between Cruxton and Southover and through Frampton Park.
Hills: There are some moderately steep inclines on the route.

YOUNG & INEXPERIENCED CYCLISTS

While there are traffic-free and off-road sections from Cruxton to Southover and a private/farm road through Frampton Park, care is needed along the A37 pavement sections, particularly where there is no verge. The country lane between Muckleford and Bradford Peverell is narrow, with blind spots and an incline.

REFRESHMENTS

- Numerous picnicking opportunities on village greens and along River Frome.
- Maiden Newton: cafe, pub, convenience store, fish and chip shop, restaurant.
- Stratton: pub with adjacent playground.
- Charminster: two pubs, one with a riverside garden and adjacent playground.
- Burton: pub with playground.
- Lots of choice in Dorchester.

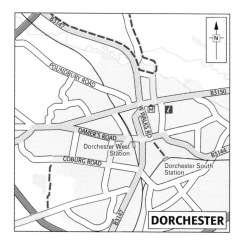

THINGS TO SEE & DO

- **Frome Vauchurch:** picturesque village on the banks of the River Frome, with the tiny church of St Francis; www.maidennewton.info
- **Nunnery Mead Nature Reserve, Southover:** water meadows, remains of a medieval village and site of a Roman villa; 01305 816546; www.dorsetwildlifetrust.org.uk/nunnery_mead_reserve
- **Wolfeton House, Dorchester:** fine early Tudor and Elizabethan manor house set in water meadows; open to groups by appointment through the year; 01305 263500; www.hha.org.uk

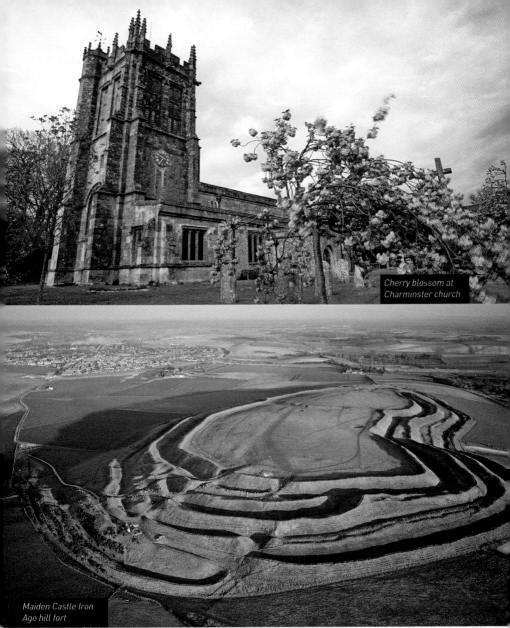

Cherry blossom at
Charminster church

Maiden Castle Iron
Age hill fort

- **Burton:** appealing village with views of Poundbury, Poundbury Hillfort and Dorchester.
- **Teddy Bear House, Dorchester:** museum and unique exhibition of human-sized teddy bears; 01305 263200; www.teddybearmuseum.co.uk

- **Poundbury:** model town and urban extension to Dorchester, pioneered by The Prince of Wales; www.duchyofcornwall.org/designanddevelopment_poundbury.htm
- **Maiden Castle, near Dorchester:** massive Iron Age hillfort; www.maidencastle.com

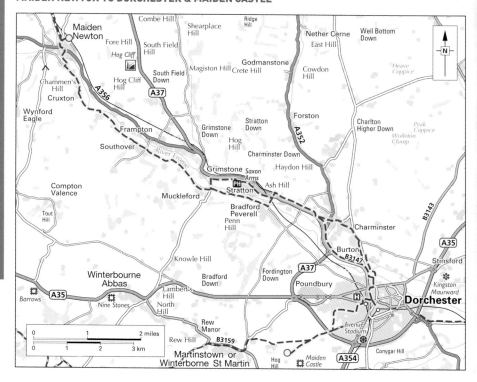

- Hardy's Cottage, Higher Bockhampton, near Dorchester: birthplace and home of Thomas Hardy; 01305 262366; www.nationaltrust.org.uk

TRAIN STATIONS

Maiden Newton; Dorchester West; Dorchester South.

BIKE HIRE

- Cycloan, Dorchester: 01305 251521; www.cycloan.co.uk
- Dorchester Cycles, Dorchester: 01305 268787; www.dorchestercycles.co.uk

FURTHER INFORMATION

- To view or print National Cycle Network routes, visit www.sustrans.org.uk
- Maps for this area are available to buy from www.sustransshop.co.uk
- Dorchester Tourist Information: 01305 267992; www.westdorset.com

ROUTE DESCRIPTION

Pick up National Route 26 at the bottom of the road at Maiden Newton train station. At the four-way junction, go left into the village (not right to Cattistock). Turn left by the convenience store, then immediately after the narrow, traffic-calmed section, turn right down Frome Lane.

After 4 miles (6.5km), at Muckleford crossroads, either take the primary route straight on via Bradford Peverell, or go left to the A37, which has a wide cycle pavement, to Stratton. Both routes meet 1.5 miles (2.5km) further along the A37.

One mile (1.6km) on, where Route 26 turns left to Charminster, you can go straight on to Dorchester – an easy but less picturesque route alongside the A37.

In Dorchester, Route 26 is only signposted to the High Street at present, so turn right, then left at the Top o' Town roundabout, then branch left along West Walks Road, skirting the Borough Gardens. At the end, go right and

'Dorset Martyrs' by Elizabeth Frink

cross Cornwall Road. Dorchester West station offers a direct train service back to Maiden Newton. Nearby Dorchester South station has services to Weymouth and London.

To complete the route to Maiden Castle, take Damers Road, then immediately after passing under the railway bridge, branch left along Dagmar Road. Turn left onto Maud Road, then second right onto Coburg Road.

Immediately after the leisure centre, a traffic-free path left of the rugby club gates leads down to Maiden Castle Road, now signposted as National Route 2.

NEARBY CYCLE ROUTES
National Route 2 from Maiden Castle is open from Dorchester to Lyme Regis and can be followed east to Wareham and Corfe Castle.

RODWELL TRAIL – WEYMOUTH TO PORTLAND

The Rodwell Trail connects Weymouth to Portland and is a pleasant route along the course of a dismantled railway. It stops at the Ferrybridge Inn on the Portland Road, and currently onward travel to Portland Bill is recommended only for experienced cyclists.

Some people have called the Isle of Portland Dorset's very own Rock of Gibraltar; a limestone peninsula jutting 4 miles (6.5km) out into the English Channel. The area has been heavily quarried over many centuries – Portland stone is highly prized, and has been used for many important public buildings, including St Paul's Cathedral, Buckingham Palace and even the headquarters of the United Nations in New York.

Portland Castle was built by Henry VIII in the 16th century to protect Weymouth against possible attack from France and Spain. In the Victorian era, it was the private residence of Charles Mannering, who was responsible for building the breakwater harbour, the largest of its kind in the world. The harbour is a popular spot for windsurfing and sailing, and will host sailing events in the 2012 Olympics.

ROUTE INFORMATION

Route: 26
Start: The Esplanade, Weymouth.
Finish: Ferrybridge Inn, at the Weymouth end of Portland Road.
Distance: 2.5 miles (4km).
Grade: Easy.
Surface: Tarmac.
Hills: None.

YOUNG & INEXPERIENCED CYCLISTS

The trail itself is ideal for novices and young children. Continuing on to Portland Bill, the cyclepath is narrow and adjacent to the road, with fast-moving traffic between Southwell and Portland Bill, and a very steep section through Fortuneswell.

Portland Bill lighthouse, a local landmark

REFRESHMENTS
- Cafe on old Castle Road next to Sandsfoot Castle (seasonal opening).
- Ferrybridge Inn, Weymouth.

THINGS TO SEE & DO
- Radipole Lake, Weymouth: nature reserve, with a good bird-watching site in the centre of the town; www.rspb.org.uk

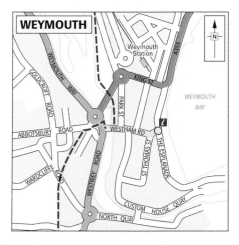

- Sandsfoot Castle and Gardens: remains of castle, which dates back to 1539; beach close by; www.weymouth.gov.uk
- Whitehead's Torpedo Factory: built in 1891 by the 'father' of the underwater torpedo, Robert Whitehead; www.weymouth.gov.uk
- Portland Castle: 16th-century fortress overlooking Portland harbour; can be seen from the end of the Trail but access requires you to continue on the busy Portland Road alongside Chesil Beach; www.english-heritage.org.uk

TRAIN STATIONS
Weymouth.

BIKE HIRE
- Weymouth Bike Hire: 01305 834951; www.weymouthbikehire.com

FURTHER INFORMATION
- To view or print National Cycle Network routes, visit www.sustrans.org.uk
- Maps for this area are available to buy from www.sustransshop.co.uk

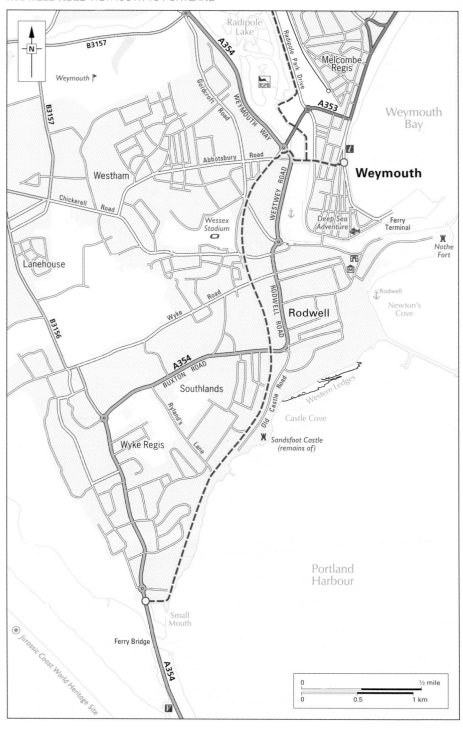

DOGS CHIPS SOFT ICE CREAM HOT DOGS TEA SOFT COFFEE DRINKS CHIPS CANDY FLOSS SWEETS SOFT ICE CREAM

Relaxing on Weymouth beach

- **Weymouth Tourist Information:**
  01305 785747; www.visitweymouth.co.uk

ROUTE DESCRIPTION

From King's Statue on the Esplanade in Weymouth, take Westham Road to the bridge by the marina. Cross it and continue straight, taking the underpass under the A354 to reach Abbotsbury Road.

Alternatively, from the Swannery car park, go under Swannery Bridge and along the Backwater to reach Westham Bridge and follow the route as above.

From Abbotsbury Road, cycle along the path until you reach Newstead Road, where you will have to leave and rejoin the trail (Sustrans is currently working on a scheme that will solve this problem).

Shortly after this you will pass the World War II gun emplacement viewing point. At Wyke Road, you go through a tunnel and then pass by what used to be Rodwell train station. At Sandsfoot Halt, you could take a detour to Sandsfoot Castle and Gardens. A little further on, there are great views of Portland Harbour from the sailing club. Towards the end of the trail, you pass the site of Whitehead's Torpedo Factory. The trail ends at the Ferry Bridge Inn on Portland Road.

NEARBY CYCLE ROUTES

National Route 2 goes from Wareham via Dorchester to Axminster. From Dorchester, National Route 26 goes north to Castle Cary.

POOLE TO RINGWOOD

This ride makes the connection between the coast and the open downs between Poole and the New Forest, as well as routes north to Fordingbridge and Salisbury. The ride is based around the Castleman Trail, named after the railway along which it runs. Opened in 1847 to connect Southampton and Dorchester, the railway was nicknamed Castleman's Corkscrew after the Wimborne solicitor who promoted the line and its circuitous route. Only a year later it was taken over by the London & South Western Railway, and then, in 1888, it was effectively bypassed by the new direct line from Brockenhurst to Bournemouth and Poole. But for all that it survived as a branch line until the Beeching years, finally closing in 1966.

There is also something of a challenge, both for Sustrans and for riders, because sections remain to be brought to their full completion in parts of Wimborne Minster. Poole, though, has a fairly extensive network of cycle routes, as well as harbours and miles of waterfront. It deserves to be a popular cycling area.

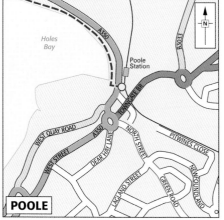

ROUTE INFORMATION
National Route: 25, Regional Route 69
Start: Poole train station or High Street.
Finish: Ringwood town centre.
Distance: 19 miles (30km).
Grade: Medium. The route is almost flat with extensive sections of railway path but it does require some navigational skills through Wimborne Minster.
Surface: Mostly smooth stone on the railway path sections.
Hills: Almost entirely flat.

YOUNG & INEXPERIENCED CYCLISTS
The Castleman Trail through Poole is particularly suitable for families, as is the Holes Bay route to Upton Country Park, provided care is taken at road crossings. A temporary diversion through Wimborne follows roads, some of which may be busy.

REFRESHMENTS
- Lots of choice in Poole.
- Frampton Cafe/Bar, Ringwood.

THINGS TO SEE & DO
- **Poole Museum:** brings to life the story of ships, boat and trade in the town, and the beginnings of the harbour, plus much more;

01202 262600; www.boroughofpoole.com
- **Poole Quay:** haven of restaurants and magnificent yachts in a lively and friendly environment; www.poolequay.com
- **Upton Country Park:** over 100 acres of garden, open parkland, woodland and the Grade II listed Upton House, which is open to the public on certain Sundays throughout the year; 01202 633555; www.uptoncountrypark.org
- **Brownsea Island, Poole Harbour:** famous for its red squirrels, wading birds and peacocks; www.nationaltrust.org.uk; reached by Brownsea Island Ferries from Poole Quay; 01202 707744;

Poole's Old Customs House is now a cafe

RINGWOOD

Sandbanks and Brownsea Island

www.brownseaislandferries.com

- Avon Heath Country Park, near Ringwod: Dorset's largest country park and a Site of Special Scientific Interest (SSSI); 01425 478470; 01425 478082; www.dorsetforyou.com

TRAIN STATIONS
Poole.

BIKE HIRE
- Front Bike Hire, Bournemouth: 01202 557007; www.front-bike-hire.co.uk

- Forest Leisure Cycling, Burley: 01425 403584; www.forestleisurecycling.co.uk

FURTHER INFORMATION
- To view or print National Cycle Network routes, visit www.sustrans.org.uk
- Maps for this area are available to buy from www.sustransshop.co.uk
- Castleman Trail Way map: www.dorsetforyou.com

ROUTE DESCRIPTION
Starting from either Poole train station or High Street, cross over the main road to the waterside and follow the Heritage Cycle Route around Holes Bay to Upton House & Country Park. Turn north here on the Roman road, which involves a rather tricky crossing of the

This ride goes to Ringwood, on the edge of the New Forest

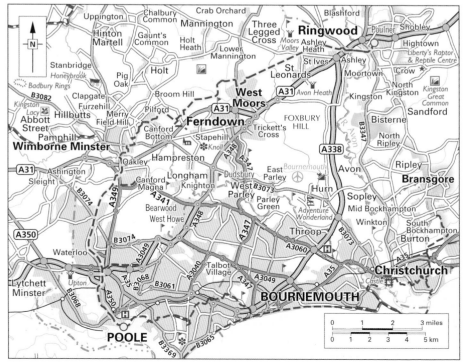

Stained glass in the
Minster at Wimborne

A35 junction. After half a mile (0.8km), bear right on the line of an old railway to join the Castleman Trail, which is a well-defined greenway running beside Broadstone Way, which itself was built on the line of the old railway. Pass through the Broadstone subways and, shortly, by the golf club, you will be on the railway path proper, called the Castleman Trail Way. This continues north to just before the River Stour, where the railway is lost and a new roadside path leads to the wonderful new bridge over the Stour. From here until you rejoin the railway path, the route is unsigned so you must make your way along roads, some of which may be busy. Sustrans hopes to sign a route at some stage. From the B3073 turn right onto Station Road, pass by the Hydroplan to the rear of the former Wimborne Station and take a short cut along a narrow footpath to reach Churchill Road. Turn left onto Barnes Crescent, then right onto Gordon Road. Turn right onto Leigh Road, the B3073, which may be busy. Turn left onto North Leigh Lane, then right onto Leigh Lane. At the end of Leigh Lane, walk your bike along a footpath to Park Homer Road.

Follow this to the left. Turn right onto Middlehill Road, then left onto Cannon Hill Road. The traffic-free route recommences at the end of Cannon Hill Road, signed with the Castleman logo, first running through Cannon Hill Plantation, then beside Udden's then beside Uddens Water, finally winding around into West Moors. Here, join Station Road, turn right and then third left, called Moorlands Road. Halfway down, turn left to join the railway path through to Ringwood, under the main road and over a number of low viaducts crossing the Test Valley. Just before the third viaduct, turn left into Riverside and go north into Ringwood town.

NEARBY CYCLE ROUTES
At Ringwood, on the edge of the New Forest, you can pick up roads and tracks for days of cycling. Start by crossing the A31 to the forest entrance at Linford. At Poole, a route goes back along roads on the east side of Poole Harbour to reach the Poole & Bournemouth Promenade. You can also take a ferry to Sandbanks, then pick up a chain ferry to Studland and work a route through to Wareham.

POOLE BAY – SANDBANKS TO CHRISTCHURCH HARBOUR

The seafront around Poole Bay must be one of the finest in the country. It offers magnificent views across to Studland, is backed by Canford Cliffs and pierced by a number of chines – ravines of shaded gardens stretching up to a mile (1.6km) inland.

The seafront is also notable for its local council taking a pragmatic view to allow cycling over its whole length, except during the peak season between 10am and 6pm in July and August. This welcome approach has given local people access to a magnificent resource, which stretches almost all the way from the Sandbanks Ferry at Purbeck to the Mudeford Ferry, which takes you across Christchurch Harbour for a route in the New Forest. This initiative has proved invaluable in demonstrating how promenades can accommodate a wider range of activities than was ever thought possible in their 1950s heyday. Then they were packed with daytrippers arriving by train, but soon their numbers declined with the explosion of private car use, which opened up many more destinations, and then there came cheap air travel to Mediterranean sunshine.

ROUTE INFORMATION
National Route: 2
Start: Sandbanks Ferry, Studland.
Finish: Mudeford Ferry, Christchurch Harbour.
Distance: 11 miles (17.5km).
Grade: Easy, but note that it is best done with the wind behind you.
Surface: Asphalt promenade throughout, but watch out for wind-blown sand out of season.

Metal marker by David Mayne

Hills: None.

YOUNG & INEXPERIENCED CYCLISTS
The whole route is useful for families, but note that the mile (1.6km) to the Sandbanks Ferry is on the main ferry road, which is busy at peak times. However, it does make you feel rather wonderful sailing past the traffic queues and reaching the ferry without delay!

REFRESHMENTS
- Lots of choice in Bournemouth.
- The Seafarer Beach Cafe, Sandbanks.
- Branksome Beach Bistro.
- Brewers Fayre pub, Boscombe Pier.
- Various options in Southbourne, including The Beach House Cafe.

THINGS TO SEE & DO
- For Poole attractions, see the Poole & Ringwood route, page 98.
- **Branksome Chine Beach:** clean water and sandy beach, ideal for even the smallest of children; www.pooleview.co.uk/beach/bchine.htm
- **Liberty's Owl, Raptor and Reptile Centre, Ringwood:** home to a large collection of birds of prey (eagles, owls and vultures), along with many well-known and popular reptiles

Bournemouth pier from West Cliff beach

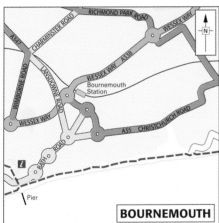

BOURNEMOUTH

CHRISTCHURCH HARBOUR

(snakes, lizards and tortoises);
01425 476487; www.libertyscentre.co.uk
- **The Bournemouth Eye:** helium balloon flight rising to 152m (500ft), offering spectacular views of 7 miles (11km) of Jurassic coastline, encompassing Poole Harbour, the Isle of Wight and 20 miles (32km) around Bournemouth: 01202 314539; www.bournemouthballoon.com
- **Bournemouth Pier:** home to the Pier Theatre; fantastic views of the coastline; 01202 306126; www.thebournemouthpier.homestead.com

TRAIN STATIONS

Parkstone; Branksome; Bournemouth; Pokesdown; Christchurch.

BIKE HIRE
- Forest Leisure Cycles, Bournemouth: 01202 424945; www.flcuk.com
- Front Bike Hire, Bournemouth: 01202 557007; www.front-bike-hire.co.uk

FURTHER INFORMATION
- To view or print National Cycle Network routes, visit www.sustrans.org.uk

Beach huts on Bournemouth Promenade

- Maps for this area are available to buy from www.sustransshop.co.uk
- Bournemouth Tourist Information: 0845 051 1700; www.bournemouth.co.uk
- Bournemouth to Swanage ferry: 01929 450203; www.sandbanksferry.co.uk
- Mudeford ferry: 07968 334441; www.mudefordferry.co.uk

ROUTE DESCRIPTION

Coming off the Sandbanks Ferry, cycle lanes take you around a one-way system. Follow Banks Road overlooking Poole Harbour, turn right onto Shore Road and cycle to the end for the Promenade. Remember that in July and August there are cycling restrictions in place between 10am and 6pm over the 3 miles (5km) to Bournemouth Pier, so set off early! Between Bournemouth and Boscombe Piers, cycling is allowed throughout the year, while further east the seasonal restriction applies again. However, at Boscombe Pier you can readily climb the hill to follow Boscombe Overcliff Road, which although not adjacent to the beach has the compensation of excellent views. At the eastern end of Poole Bay, pick up the Southbourne Coast Road and turn right past the golf course to join the path at the foot of Hengistbury Head for the Mudeford Ferry. This operates from Easter until the end of October.

NEARBY CYCLE ROUTES

This Promenade is a key part of National Route 2, the South Coast Route. To the west, various local routes are signposted as part of the Purbeck Cycle Network. To the east, you can follow the completed Route 2 through Christchurch on the way to the New Forest, where there is an extensive network of very attractive cycle routes.

In Bournemouth itself, the Bourne Valley Greenway leads inland from the Pier to the town centre, past the Lower, Middle and Upper Gardens – they were once known as the Upper, Middle and Lower Pleasure Gardens!

FOREST OF DEAN CIRCUIT

The Forest of Dean is something of a magnet for cyclists. It has hundreds of miles of good forest roads and old railways and tramways, all of which are open to cyclists. This 11-mile (17.5-km) signposted circuit is a family ride that takes you through the heart of the forest and past the remains of the iron workings, collieries and quarries that make this such an interesting place. At the same time, it is both a working forest and an area with a wonderfully rich and varied wildlife, which both need to be respected. Certain areas, green paths and nature reserves are therefore not all accessible to bicycles.

The Forestry Commission has long promoted cycling in many of their forests and, without their support, quite a few routes on the National Cycle Network would be incomplete. At the same time, Sustrans has endeavoured to support the Forestry Commission by creating cycling routes from the nearest towns to the forests. In this case, the routes planned from Chepstow, Monmouth, Ross-on-Wye and Gloucester are still being developed, and the best access to the Forest of Dean remains by car, although good railway paths are open to Coleford, Upper Lydbrook and Cinderford.

ROUTE INFORMATION
National Route: 42
Start: Beechenhurst car park.
Finish: Beechenhurst car park.
Distance: 11 miles (17.5km).
Additional links, to Coleford: 4.5 miles (7km) extra; to Upper Lydford: 2 miles (3km) extra.
Grade: Easy.
Surface: Stone.
Hills: Generally flat; the route is mostly on old railways and linking forest roads.

YOUNG & INEXPERIENCED CYCLISTS
The route is traffic-free throughout,except for a few road crossings.

REFRESHMENTS
• Cafe in Beechenhurst.
• Pubs and cafes in Cinderford and Coleford.

• The Woodman pub, Parkend.

THINGS TO SEE & DO
• Nagshead Nature Reserve, Forest of Dean: mainly oak woodland, at its most beautiful in spring; visitor centre; hides are open all year round; managed by the Forestry Commission and RSPB; 01594 833057; www.forestry.gov.uk
• Speech House Woodland, near Cinderford: built in 1676 by the King as a 'court', where local people could have their say; 01594 833057; www.forestry.gov.uk
• Mallards Pike: lakes constructed by the Forestry Commission for leisure use; family cycle route passes close by; three walking trails, a running trail and ramblers routes; 01594 833057; www.visitforestry.gov.uk
• Soudley Ponds, Forest of Dean: haven for wildlife, especially birds and dragonflies; picnic area and Blaize Bailey viewpoint; www.forestry.gov.uk
• New Fancy: old spoil heap, formerly the site of the New Fancy coal mine; spectacular views across the New Forest and an ideal place to watch birds of prey soaring above the woodland; there is easy access to the cycleways from here.

Pedalabikeaway Centre, Cannop Valley

Cyclists in the Cannop Valley

- Forest of Dean Sculpture Trail: 01594 833057; www.forestofdean-sculpture.org.uk

BIKE HIRE

- Pedalabikeaway Cycle Centre, Cannop Valley: 01594 860065; www.pedalabikeaway.com

FURTHER INFORMATION

- To view or print National Cycle Network routes, visit www.sustrans.org.uk
- Maps for this area are available to buy from www.sustransshop.co.uk
- Forest of Dean Tourist Information: 01594 833057; www.forestofdean.co.uk

Bluebells in the
Forest of Dean

ROUTE DESCRIPTION

You can go either way around the central trail,
although clockwise takes advantage of the
easier railway gradient. Make sure you pick up
a forest cycle route map before you start, as
this gives the location of a series of numbered
location posts scattered through the whole
forest. These are very useful in orientating
yourself – one part of the forest can look very
much like somewhere else you have passed
through earlier.

About half a mile (0.8km) north of the
Beechenhurst car park, the branch line path to
Upper Lydbrook veers off to the left. This route

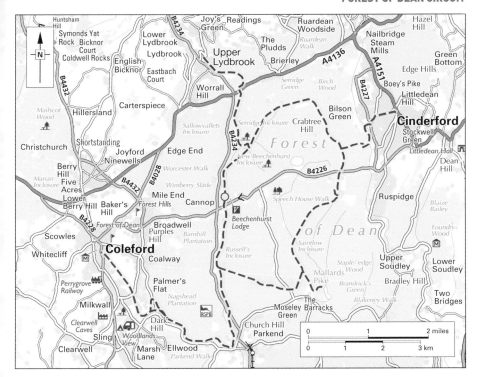

is notable for the initiative of local freeminers to reopen the Mirystock Tunnel under the main road. At the southern end of the forest circuit, you can turn south down the railway to Parkend (for the Forest of Dean Steam Railway to Lydney) and follow yet another old railway route to Coleford – the main town of the Forest.

NEARBY CYCLE ROUTES

From Cinderford, you might like to explore the planned continuation of National Route 42, via more forest tramways, past Drybrook and then the beautiful country lanes past Hope Mansell to Ross-on-Wye. Downstream at Monmouth you will find the Peregrine Path, which runs on the old railway for 5 miles (8km) beside the River Wye to Symonds Yat.

Wild boar in the Forest of Dean

A choice of pleasant cycle routes

GLOUCESTER TO SLIMBRIDGE WILDFOWL & WETLAND TRUST (WWT)

To the south of the cathedral city of Gloucester, the towpath of the Gloucester & Sharpness Canal offers an excellent escape route into the countryside, with the Cotswold Hills running parallel away to the east. Opened in 1827 to bypass a treacherous and winding stretch of the River Severn, the canal was at the time the widest and deepest in the country. This greatly increased construction costs but with the result that the canal remains in use today, and Sharpness Docks and Gloucester are still commercial ports accessible by ocean-going vessels, as all its road crossings are opening bridges.

From the Rea Bridge, quiet lanes with fine views across the Severn to the Forest of Dean take you to Frampton on Severn, with its vast village green, attractive old houses, pubs and shops. South from here, an improved section of the towpath leads directly to Shepherd's Patch and the minor road to Slimbridge Wildfowl & Wetlands Trust, one of the most important wildfowl sites in Britain.

ROUTE INFORMATION
National Route: 41
Start: Gloucester Docks (Llanthony Road), in the heart of the city.
Finish: Slimbridge Wildfowl & Wetlands Trust.
Distance: 14 miles (22.5km).
Grade: Easy.
Surface: Good-quality stone towpath from

Gloucester to Rea Bridge, and quiet lanes to Frampton on Severn.
Hills: Gentle hills.

YOUNG & INEXPERIENCED CYCLISTS
The towpath section from the centre of Gloucester to Rea Bridge is traffic-free. The lanes south from Rea Bridge to Frampton on Severn have very little traffic.

REFRESHMENTS
- Lots of choice in the centre of Gloucester.
- Pilot Inn, Hardwicke.
- The Anchor Inn, Epney.
- Ship Inn, Upper Framilode.
- Cafes at the Canal Preservation Trust at Saul and at Shepherds Patch.
- The Bell Inn, village shops and tea rooms at Frampton on Severn.
- Tudor Arms, Slimbridge.
- Cafe at the Wildfowl & Wetlands Trust, Slimbridge.

THINGS TO SEE & DO
- Gloucester Cathedral: 01452 521957; www.gloucestercathedral.org.uk
- National Waterways Museum: 01452 318200; www.nwm.org.uk

Gloucester Cathedral

Flamingos at Slimbridge

Gloucester's historic docklands

- **Gloucester Docks:**
  www.visit-gloucestershire.co.uk
- **Frampton Court Estate, Frampton-on-Severn:** includes historic Frampton Court, The Manor, The Wool Barn and Court Lake; www.framptoncourtestate.co.uk
- **Wildfowl & Wetlands Trust HQ, Slimbridge:** home to the world's largest collection of swans, geese and ducks; ample bike parking and impressive visitor centre and cafe; 01453 891900; www.wwt.org.uk
- **Severn Bore:** a form of tidal wave, caused by each incoming tide funnelling into shallower water, which can result in a bore up to 2m (6.5ft) high on spring tides, travelling at speeds of 10 miles/hour (16km/h). The road at Stonebench is an excellent site to see the Bore at its most impressive. Check times in advance; 01452 421188; www.environment-agency.gov.uk

GLOUCESTER TO SLIMBRIDGE WWT

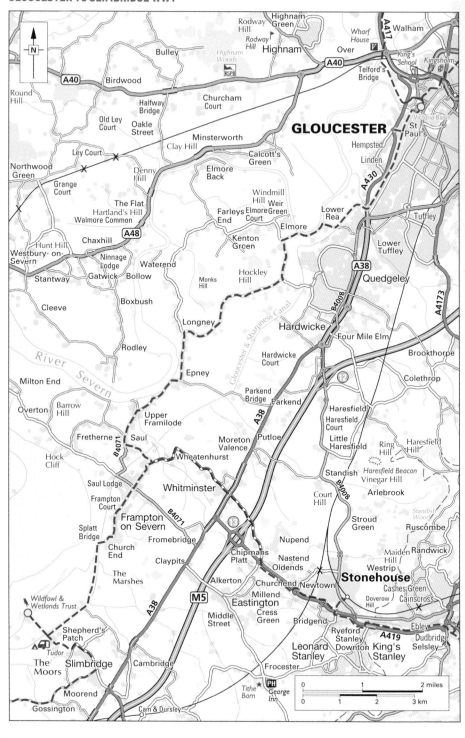

The village green at Frampton on Severn

TRAIN STATIONS
Gloucester; Cam & Dursley.

FURTHER INFORMATION
- To view or print National Cycle Network routes, visit www.sustrans.org.uk
- Maps for this area are available to buy from www.sustransshop.co.uk
- Gloucester Tourist Information: 01452 396572; www.gloucester.gov.uk/tourism

ROUTE DESCRIPTION
From Llanthony Road at the Gloucester Docks, take the traffic-free path, on the west of the water, southwards. You follow this towpath through the outskirts of Gloucester towards the residential area of Quedgeley. Where the path ramps up to Rea bridge after passing under the new bridge carrying the Gloucester bypass, join the waymarked National Route 41 on quiet lanes. Quedgeley itself has an extensive network of dedicated cycle routes.

The route will take you through the village of Frampton on Severn, from where you rejoin the canal towpath to Slimbridge and the Wildfowl & Wetlands Trust. From here, you can continue on minor roads through Slimbridge village to Cam & Dursley train station and catch a train back to Gloucester.

NEARBY CYCLE ROUTES
This route is on National Route 41, which runs from Bristol to Gloucester, and will eventually continue to Stratford-upon-Avon and Rugby.

Other waymarked or traffic-free rides include:
- National Route 42 from Gloucester Docks to the village of Highnam, or from Telford's Over Bridge follow Route 45 by the river to Maisemore. From here, quiet lanes lead north towards Tewkesbury.
- The Stroud Valleys Cycle Trail, a 5-mile (8-km) railway path from Stonehouse to Nailsworth (see page 114). The trail is part of National Route 45 to Cirencester, beyond which there are several traffic-free trails in Cotswold Water Park, to the south of Cirencester.

STONEHOUSE & STROUD TO NAILSWORTH & KEMBLE

One of the challenges of cycling through the Cotswolds is finding good ways up its western escarpment – all the easiest routes are occupied by main roads. On this ride, you follow a combination of the Stroudwater Canal, the old branch line to Nailsworth and a climb up the hill on a back road to Minchinhampton, which makes for a sufficiently out-of-the-way route, of little interest to motorists. The ride then bowls along the wide open spaces of the Cotswolds, assuming you have a west wind behind you, to Kemble station. For your return trip, you could drop down into the Golden Valley and explore the towpath back to Stroud, along a canal, which, it is hoped, will reopen to boats through the Sapperton tunnel and all the way to Lechlade for the Thames.

ROUTE INFORMATION
National Route: 45
Start: Stonehouse train station.
Finish: Kemble train station.
Distance: 14 miles (22.5km).
Grade: Mostly easy.
Surface: Mostly tarmac roads and good stone paths.
Hills: There is a long climb up to Minchinhampton.

YOUNG & INEXPERIENCED CYCLISTS
The Nailsworth Railway Path is a good place to start cycling. The overall route is mostly on quiet lanes but there are one or two main road crossings where care is needed, including over the Fosse Way on the approach to Kemble.

REFRESHMENTS
• Lots of choice in Stonehouse, Stroud and Nailsworth.

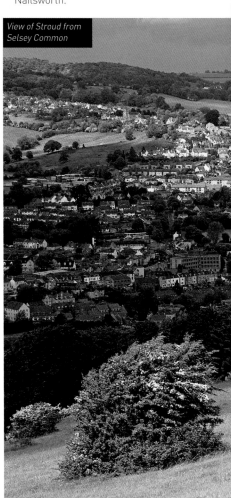
View of Stroud from Selsey Common

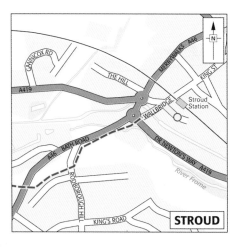

ACKNOWLEDGEMENTS

John Grimshaw would like to thank: Adrian Roper, Alistair Millington, Rupert Crosbee, Peter Grainger, Simon Murray, Kim Goonesekera, Patrick Tully, Alan K Will, Alastair Goldie, Andy Parsons, Chris Vincent, David Parkin, Derek White, Duncan Day, Geoff Pell, Jan Gannaway, Janice Laird, John and Glynne Miller, John Vuagniaux, Lewis Lawton, Matt Brooks, Michael Keatinge, Nick Stedman, Nigel Stanton, Peter Hobbs, Richard Barnes, Richard Dyson, Robert Grundy, Eric Pinch, Tim Musk, Tony Fitt.

The Automobile Association wishes to thank the following photographers and organisations for their assistance in the preparation of this book.

Abbreviations for the picture credits are as follows – (t) top; (b) bottom; (l) left; (r) right; (c) centre; (dps) double page spread; (AA) AA World Travel Library

Trade Cover: t Porthcurno Beach, Land's End, Cornwall, AA/J Wood; b Smiling girl, Jon Bewley/Sustrans

Special Sales Cover: t St Ives harbour at low tide, AA/John Wood; b Young couple cycling through a meadow, Digital Vision/Getty

3bl Jon Bewley/Sustrans; 3br AA/Adam Burton; 4 Jon Bewley/Sustrans; 5i AA/John Wood; 5ii AA/Roger Moss; 5iii AA/Rupert Tenison; 5iv AA/Linda Whitwam; 6-7 AA/Adam Burton; 7i AA/Caroline Jones; 7ii AA/Nigel Hicks; 7iii Terry Wall/Alamy; 7iv AA/Caroline Jones; 7bc Jon Bewley/Sustrans; 11tl Jon Bewley/Sustrans; 11tr Jon Bewley/Sustrans; 11c Jon Bewley/Sustrans; 11bc Andy Huntley/Sustrans; 11br Pru Comben/Sustrans; 13t Jon Bewley/Sustrans; 13c Nicola Jones/Sustrans; 13b Jon Bewley/Sustrans; 14-15 AA/Caroline Jones; 16 AA/Caroline Jones; 19 Kevin Britland/Alamy; 21 AA/John Wood; 23 AA/Roger Moss; 25 AA/John Wood; 26 John Grimshaw/Sustrans; 27 AA/Rupert Tenison; 29t AA/John Wood; 29c AA/Neil Ray; 31 AA/Nigel Hicks; 33t AA/Nigel Hicks; 33c AA/Peter Baker; 34 Anthea Truby/Sustrans; 35 Sheila Cheatle/Sustrans; 37t AA/Nigel Hicks; 37c AA/Nigel Hicks; 39l AA/Nigel Hicks; 39r AA/Guy Edwardes; 41t AA/Nigel Hicks; 41c Jon Bewley/Sustrans; 43 AA/Nigel Hicks; 45 Marc Hill/Alamy; 46-47b Globuss Images/Alamy; 47t Apex News and Pictures Agency/Alamy; 49 Marc Hill/Alamy; 50 Jon Bewley/Sustrans; 51t AA/Nigel Hicks; 51c AA/Nigel Hicks; 52 John Grimshaw/Sustrans; 53 ICP/Alamy; 54-55 AA/Nigel Hicks; 57tl Victor Watts/Alamy; 57tr Graham Clarke/Alamy; 57c Tony Ambrose/Sustrans; 59t Lynne Evans/Alamy; 59b Mark Bolton Photography/Alamy; 61 Lynne Evans/Alamy; 62-63 AA/Richard Ireland; 65 AA/Caroline Jones; 67t AA/James Tims; 67c Jon Bewley/Sustrans; 69t AA/James Tims; 69c AA/James Tims; 71 Stephen Shepherd/Alamy; 73 John Grimshaw/Sustrans; 75tl AA/Caroline Jones; 75tr AA/Dennis Kelsall; 79 AA/Caroline Jones; 80 AA/Dennis Kelsall; 81l Nick Turner/Sustrans; 81r AA/Michael Moody; 82 Jim McEwen/Sustrans; 83 Tim Gander/Alamy; 85t Jon Bewley/Sustrans; 85b Sean Malyon/Alamy; 86-87b AA/Caroline Jones; 87t Sustrans; 89t Steve Morgan/Sustrans; 89b AA/Michael Moody; 91t Steve Atkins Photography/Alamy; 91b Skyscan Photolibrary/Alamy; 93 AA/Richard Ireland; 94-95 AA/Max Jourdan; 97 AA/Max Jourdan; 99t Robert Harding Picture Library Ltd/Alamy; 99c Jack Sullivan/Alamy; 100 AA/Adam Burton; 101tr Nick Lewis Photography/Alamy; 102 John Grimshaw/Sustrans; 103 AA/Adam Burton; 105 AA/Adam Burton; 106 Alan Luke/Sustrans; 107 Richard Wayman/Alamy; 108 nagelestock.com/Alamy; 109cr David J Slater/Alamy; 109br John Grimshaw/Sustrans; 110 John Grimshaw/Sustrans; 111t AA/David Hall; 111cr AA/Hugh Palmer; 113t AA/Steve Day; 113cr Jon Bewley/Sustrans; 114-115 AA/David Hall; 117tl AA/Adrian Baker; 117tr AA/Richard Ireland; 118 Jon Bewley/Sustrans; 119 AA/David Hall; 121t David J Slater/Alamy; 121c David J Slater/Alamy; 123t AA/Steve Day; 123c Jon Bewley/Sustrans; 125 AA/Michael Moody.

Every effort has been made to trace the copyright holders, and we apologise in advance for any unintentional omissions or errors. We would be pleased to apply any corrections in the following edition of this publication.

Help Sustrans to change our world
Join the charity that is making a difference today so we can all live a better tomorrow.
Sustrans is the UK's leading sustainable transport charity. Our vision is a world in which people choose to travel in ways that benefit their health and the environment. We are the charity working with children in schools, with families at home, with employers and with whole communities to enable people to travel much more by foot, bike and public transport. Sustrans is a 'doing' charity; working with many partners to bring about real change. Our thousands of supporters are enabling and helping us to change our world one mile at a time. You can too.
Join the movement today at www.sustrans.org.uk/support
Or call 0845 838 0651
sustrans
JOIN THE MOVEMENT

- The Three Horse Shoes, Frampton on Severn.
- The Kitchen, Minchinhampton.

THINGS TO SEE & DO
- Museum in the Park, Stratford Park, Stroud: a look at the story of Stroud, the Five Valleys and the wider district; 01453 763394; www.museuminthepark.org.uk
- Frocester Tithe Barn, Stroud: built in the 13th century, this is one of the most important and best-preserved barns in England; 01453 823250; www.gloucestershire.gov.uk

- Frampton Court Estate, Frampton-on-Severn: includes historic Frampton Court, The Manor, The Wool Barn and Court Lake; www.framptoncourtestate.co.uk
- Woodchester Mansion, Nailsworth: carefully preserved but unfinished Gothic masterpiece, abandoned in 1868 after 16 years of building; park with lovely woodland walks, lakes and ponds; tours available; 01453 861541; www.woodchestermansion.org.uk

TRAIN STATIONS
Stonehouse; Stroud; Kemble.

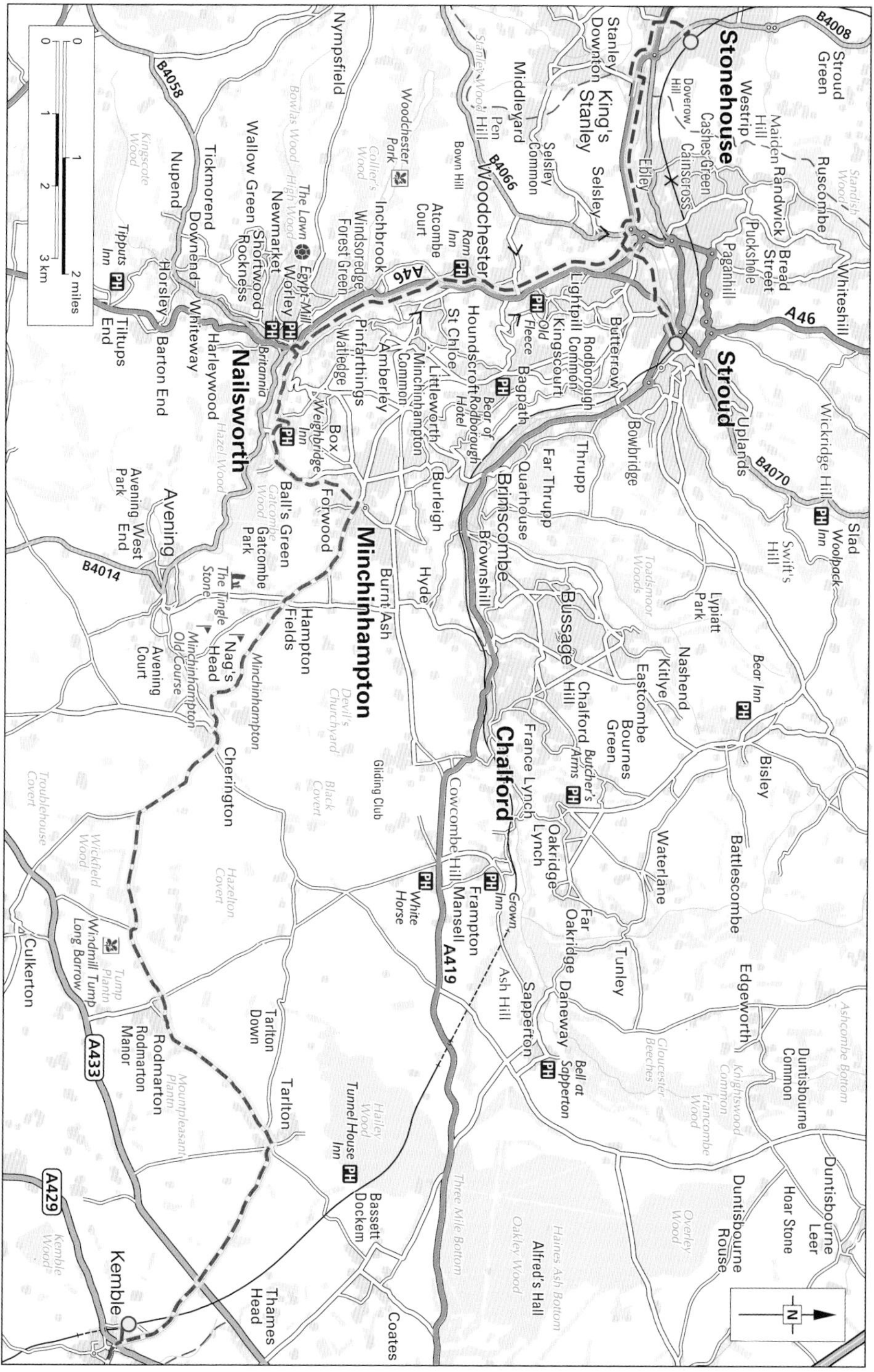
Stonehouse
Stroud
Nailsworth
Minchinhampton
Chalford
Kemble
Woodchester
King's Stanley
Avening
Bussage
Brimscombe
Sapperton
Bisley
Tarlton
Rodmarton
Cherington
Coates
Frampton Mansell
Nympsfield
B4008
B4058
B4066
A46
B4070
B4014
A419
A433
A429
0 1 2 miles
0 1 2 3 km
N

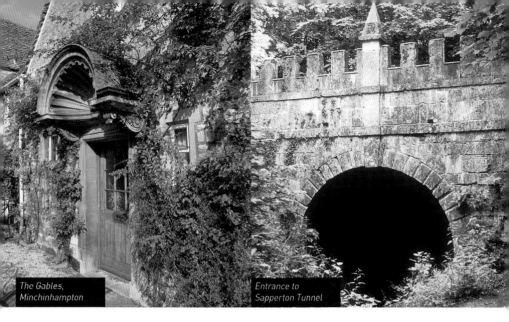

The Gables,
Minchinhampton

Entrance to
Sapperton Tunnel

BIKE HIRE
- Stonehouse Accessories, Stonehouse:
  24 hours notice required; 01453 822881
- Go By Cycle, Cirencester: 07970 419208;
  www.go-by-cycle.co.uk

FURTHER INFORMATION
- To view or print National Cycle Network
  routes, visit www.sustrans.org.uk
- Maps for this area are available to buy from
  www.sustransshop.co.uk
- Stroudwater Canal: www.waterscape.com

ROUTE DESCRIPTION
Go downhill from Stonehouse station and left at
the main road. Then turn right down Regent
Street to join the railway path, after crossing
the Bristol Road at the toucan crossing. Turn
east along the railway path and follow the signs
to Nailsworth. After half a mile (0.8km), cross
the Stroudwater Canal and join its informal
towpath for a direct route to Stroud town
centre, or turn west to work your way back
towards the Gloucester and Sharpness Ship
Canal at Saul.

The railway path is now close to the main
road, which it crosses at Dudbridge. Here,
there is a signposted path to Stroud town
centre and station, but then you are away along
the old railway line, through a short corrugated
steel tunnel and south down a wooded valley to
Nailsworth, 3 miles (5km) away. From the town
centre, follow very small roads eastwards and
climb steadily, but easily, to Minchinhampton,
Turn right before the church and follow the
road to Cherington, Rodmarton and Tarlton.
Here, you have a string of options: go straight
on for half a mile (0.8km) and you come to the
headquarters of the Severn & Thames Canal
Project, just near the mouth of Sapperton
tunnel; turn sharp left just before the village of
Tarlton and you can cycle through to Frampton
Mansell, to explore the Golden Valley back to
Stroud; or turn right for Kemble station, taking
care when crossing the Roman road, the Fosse
Way, running from Exeter to Lincoln.

NEARBY CYCLE ROUTES
From Stonehouse, National Route 45 goes west
along roadside cyclepaths and minor roads to
reach the River Severn route to Gloucester and
Slimbridge (see page 110). At Kemble, you can
easily reach Cirencester, another 5 miles (8km)
away, along busyish roads, still Route 45, then
through Cotswold Water Park and on to
Cricklade and Swindon. The route eventually
takes you to Avebury, Stonehenge, Old Sarum
and Salisbury.

COTSWOLD WATER PARK TO SWINDON

This ride is part of National Route 45, which runs from Salisbury, past Stonehenge and Avebury, via Gloucester and the Severn Valley to Shrewsbury. The ride starts at the Cotswold Water Park, which is a watery world of restored gravel pits threaded through with a maze of tracks and paths, which could make a good base for cycling. This route follows the old railway south to Cricklade and then picks up the extensive network of cycling routes in Swindon, taking you through to the leisure centre, the station and the town centre.

ROUTE INFORMATION

National Route: 45
Start: South Cerney village centre.
Finish: Swindon train station.
Distance: 15 miles (24km).
Grade: Easy.
Surface: Mostly good stone, with tarmac paths in Swindon.
Hills: None.

YOUNG & INEXPERIENCED CYCLISTS

Almost all of the route is suitable for children and novices, although Tadpole Lane on the north side of Swindon can be a little busy, and you should take care through Cricklade.

REFRESHMENTS

- The Eliot Arms, South Cerney: typical Cotswold pub-cum-hotel dating from the 16th century.
- Cricklade Fritillary Tea Room, Cricklade.
- Lots of choice in Swindon.

THINGS TO SEE & DO

- Cotswold Water Park: area of 140 lakes, set in marvellous countryside, with various activities on offer, including sailing, fishing and watersports; picturesque villages, campsites, hotels and country inns; 01793 752413; www.waterpark.org
- Cricklade Museum, Cricklade: despite its small size, the museum has more than 8,000 items in its collection; 01793 750686; www.cricklademuseum.org
- Lydiard House & Park: ancestral home of the Viscounts Bolingbroke, lying in beautiful parkland; requires a short detour through Eastlease on the west side of Swindon, where there is a network of local cycle routes; 01793 770401; www.lydiardpark.org.uk

Reed beds at the Cotswold Water Park

TRAIN STATIONS
Swindon.

BIKE HIRE
• Swindon Cycles Superstore, Upper Stratton: 01793 700105; www.swindoncycles.co.uk

FURTHER INFORMATION
• To view or print National Cycle Network routes, visit www.sustrans.org.uk
• Maps for this area are available to buy from www.sustransshop.co.uk
• Swindon Tourist Information: 01793 530328; www.visitswindon.co.uk

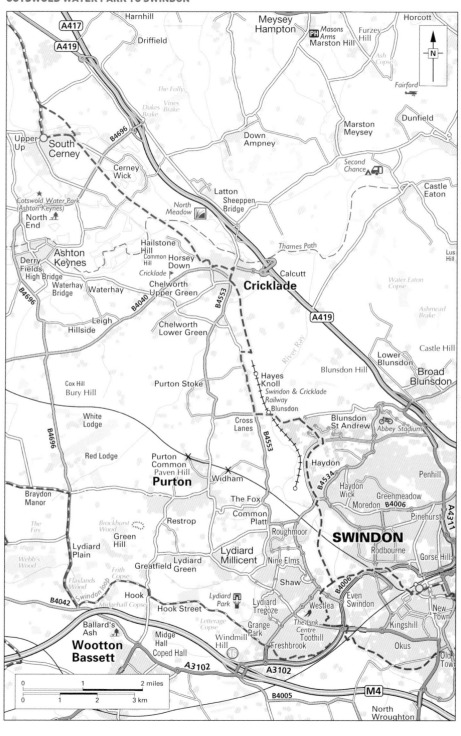

Cricklade Snakeshead Fritillary Meadow

Snakeshead Fritillary

The railway path joins the road to Cross Lanes, where you turn left to cross over the tracks for the Swindon & Cricklade Railway. Then, after half a mile (0.8km), turn right on to new cycle paths. Turn right at the main Thamesdown Drive and follow the dedicated cycle track to rejoin the railway path just by the roundabout at its end. From there its plain sailing, under the Gloucester to Swindon railway and left at the end of the path, to go east past the sewage works, and under the railway again. Cross the road at the lights, and continue under the Great Western Way along a brick-walled path, past the former locomotive works under the Bristol to Paddington mainline, and ending up at Swindon station.

NEARBY CYCLE ROUTES

There are numerous local cycle routes in Swindon, or you can go south on National Route 45 to Coate Water Country Park, the Ridgeway and Marlborough (see page 122). Route 45 north from South Cerney is signposted along the road to Siddington and Cirencester. This is only an interim route, as plans for reopening the Thames & Severn Canal will yield a much more satisfying route. From Cirencester, the route is signposted to Gloucester and beyond.

ROUTE DESCRIPTION

The railway path starts at the southeastern corner of South Cerney and is signposted to Swindon. After 2.5 miles (4km), you cross over the River Thames, which at this point is just a small stream. Cricklade is an interesting town with a notable church tower. Just beyond the roundabout at the south end of High Street, bear left onto the railway path built by Sustrans volunteers in Summer 2002.

SWINDON TO MARLBOROUGH

This ride takes you south from the centre of Swindon to the open spaces of the Marlborough Downs and makes an easy route to the Ridgeway – Britain's oldest road. Marlborough town centre is an attractive destination, and you could return via Avebury stone circles on a track that takes you past a whole landscape of littered sarsen stones.

ROUTE INFORMATION
National Routes: 45 and 482
Start: Swindon train station.
Finish: Marlborough high street.
Distance: 15 miles (24km).
Grade: Easy.
Surface: Mostly compacted stone paths and tarmac roads.
Hills: There is just one short hill at Chiseldon.

YOUNG & INEXPERIENCED CYCLISTS
Ideal as an outing for a novice, while children will probably find Coate Water Country Park, the spiral ramp over the M4 and the railway path to Chiseldon an adventure enough.

REFRESHMENTS
• Lots of choice in Swindon.
• Cafe at Queens Park, Swindon.
• The Ugly Duckling Cafe, Coate Water Country Park.
• The Plough Inn, Badbury.
• The Calley Arms, Hodson.
• Patriots Arms, Chiseldon.
• The Riverside Cafe, Marlborough.

THINGS TO SEE & DO
• Steam Museum of the Great Western Railway, Swindon Centre: tells the remarkable story of the men and women who built, operated and travelled on 'God's Wonderful Railway'; 01793 466646; www.steam-museum.org.uk uk/leisure-parkscoatewater
• Swindon Museum & Art Gallery, Old Town, Swindon: displays of local history, archaeology and the Jurassic past of Swindon; 01793 466556; www.swindon.gov.uk
• Coate Water Country Park: 56-acre reservoir

and smaller lake, which acts as flood storage lagoon; Site of Special Scientific Interest (SSSI), protecting the wildlife and wildflower meadows; 01793 490150; www.swindon.gov. uk/leisure-parkscoatewater
• Richard Jefferies Museum, Coate: features mementoes of Richard Jefferies (1848–87), one of England's most individual writers on nature and the countryside; 01793 783040; www.swindon.gov.uk/richardjefferies

TRAIN STATIONS
Swindon.

BIKE HIRE
• Swindon Cycles Superstore, Upper Stratton: 01793 700105; www.swindoncycles.co.uk
• Coate Water Country Park: booking form from 01793 490150; www.swindon.gov.uk

FURTHER INFORMATION
• To view or print National Cycle Network routes, visit www.sustrans.org.uk

Attractive houses in Marlborough

A popular stretch of Route 45

- Maps for this area are available to buy from www.sustransshop.co.uk
- **Swindon Tourist Information:** cycle maps available; 01793 530328; www.visitswindon.co.uk

ROUTE DESCRIPTION

If you have a Swindon cycling map, then there are a number of options through the town, depending upon your desire to explore. Your immediate destination is Coate Water Country Park. Starting from Swindon station, Route 45 is signposted to the left. After a few residential streets it follows paths around the infamous 'Magic Roundabout',and alongside the busy Queen's Drive. Much more interesting is to go to the shopping centre via the wide piazza through the bus station and follow Canal Street to the west. This picks up fragmentary remains of the Wiltshire & Berkshire Canal (Abingdon to Trowbridge) and then joins the Old Town Railway Path, which was a very early Sustrans project constructed with the aid of young offenders on probation. Yet another alternative from the town centre is to walk up Regent Street, and work your way east from the council offices.

Exit through the old station yard and cross left, then right over the main road to Old Mill Lane, and turn right for Coate Water Country Park. After all this, Coate Water Country Park is a sparkling jewel and you are on your way to open countryside! Follow Route 45 signs and spiral over the M4 ramp – good for photos – to rejoin the Old Town line to Marlborough. The first section to Chiseldon was built by a

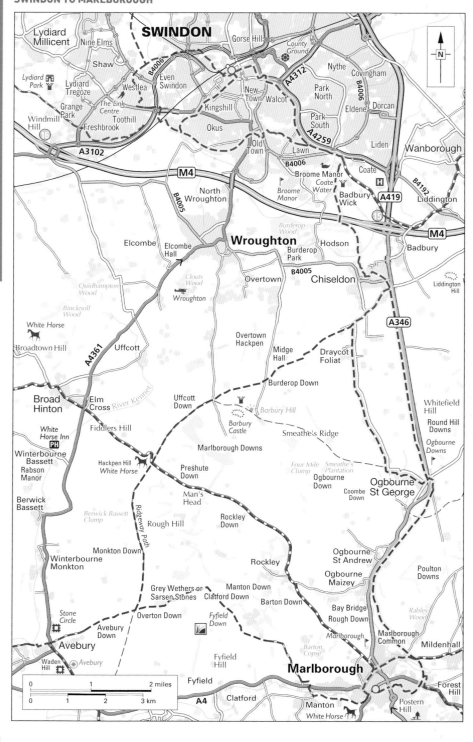

Avebury Stone Circle

Sustrans summer work camp during a gloriously hot 2002, although all their efforts failed to achieve the final link to the old station site. At present, you reach Station Road, built on the line of the old railway, via a link through the housing. The railway path runs past allotments and crosses The Ridgeway, which leads up to Barbury Castle. At this point, you can either follow The Ridgeway and, after 1 mile (1.6km), turn right down along the tarmac road to Ogbourne St George, or you can follow the fairly rough railway path, which has never been fully developed due to shortage of funds. This exactly parallels the dead-straight Roman road, A346, which this route set out to avoid. But, once at Ogbourne St George, the railway path curves away into the Chalk Downs and is an attractive approach to Marlborough itself.

NEARBY CYCLE ROUTES

You can return via the Ridgeway, which is best done if the weather is dry, along National Route 403. When you leave Marlborough, turn right at the end of the high street and then left after the college into Granham Close. At Manton, you can either go right via the Downs or straight on for the Avenue to Avebury.

Route 403 goes south through Savernake Forest to join the Kennet & Avon Canal to London. Alternatively, from Swindon you can follow Route 45 north to the Cotswold Water Park and Cirencester (see page 118).

NEXT STEPS...

We hope you have enjoyed the cycle rides in this book.

Sustrans developed the National Cycle Network to act as a catalyst for bringing cycling (and walking) back into our everyday lives. Between the 1950s and the mid 1970s cycling in the UK fell by 80%. Cycling now accounts for only about 2% of all journeys made in the UK, a fraction of what we used to achieve.

When you consider that nearly 6 in 10 car journeys are under 5 miles, it makes you wonder what the potential for increasing levels of cycling is? Evidence shows that, for local journeys under 5 miles, the majority of us could make 9 out of 10 journeys on foot, bike or public transport if there was more investment in making it possible to choose to leave the car behind.

And why not? We can all be more savvy when it comes to travel. One small step becomes one giant leap if we all start walking away from less healthy lifestyles and pedalling our way towards happier children and a low carbon world.

And that's where Sustrans comes in. Sustainable travel means carbon-reducing, energy efficient, calorie burning, money-saving travel. Here are a few things that we think make sense. If you agree, join us.

- Snail's pace – 20 mph or less on our streets where we live, go to school, shop and work – make it the norm, not just the four times a century when we get snow.

- Closer encounters – planning that focuses on good non-motorised access, so that we can reach more post offices, schools, shops, doctors and dentists without the car.

- People spaces – streets where kids can play hopscotch or football and be free-range, and where neighbours can meet and chat.

- Road revolution – build miles and miles of bike paths that don't evaporate when they meet a road.

- Find our feet – campaign for pedestrian-friendly city centres, or wide boulevards with regular pedestrian crossings and slow-moving traffic.

- Better buses – used by millions, under-invested by billions and, if affordable, reliable and pleasant to use, could make local car journeys redundant.

- More car clubs – a car club on every street corner and several for every new-build estate.

- Rewards for car-sharing – get four in a car and take more than half the cars off the road.

- Trains – more of them, more cheaply.

- Become a staycationer – and holiday at home. Mountains, beaches, culture, great beer, good food and a National Cycle Network that connects them all.

If we work towards these goals we have a chance of delivering our fair share of the 80% reduction in CO_2 by mid-century that we're now committed to by law, and some of the 100% reduction that many climate experts now consider essential.